Creativity

Unconventional
Wisdom
from 20
Accomplished
Minds

EDWARD ALBEE CHRIS BANGLE DALE CHIHULY
CHUCK CLOSE MILTON GLASER STEVEN HOLL
DAVID HALBERSTAM   JAMES ROSENQUIST
STEVE WOZNIAK ILANA GOOR NANDAN NILEKANI
DANIEL LIBESKIND ERICA JONG ROLAND HEILER
SPIKE LEE MARVIN HAMLISCH KARIM RASHID
JULIE TAYMOR KEN HEYMAN PAUL THOMPSON

Edited by **Herb Meyers** **Richard Gerstman**

palgrave
macmillan

Also by the authors:

Branding @ the digital age (eds), Palgrave Macmillan
The Visionary Package, Palgrave Macmillan

Also by Herbert Meyers:

The Marketer's Guide to Successful Package Design
(co-author Murray J. Lubliner, McGraw-Hill)

In memory of David Halberstam, journalist and
author, who graciously provided the first interview
for this book. His unconventional wisdom and
reporting of the truth when covering the Vietnam
War created a new kind of journalism.

Quotation opposite used by permission of The Society of Authors, on behalf of The Bernard Shaw Estate.

You see things; and you say "why"
but I dream things that never were; and I say "why not."
George Bernard Shaw

First published 2007 by
PALGRAVE MACMILLAN
Houndmills, Basingstoke, Hampshire RG21 6XS and
175 Fifth Avenue, New York, N.Y. 10010
Companies and representatives throughout the world

PALGRAVE MACMILLAN is the global academic imprint of the Palgrave Macmillan division of St. Martin's Press, LLC and of Palgrave Macmillan Ltd. Macmillan® is a registered trademark in the United States, United Kingdom and other countries. Palgrave is a registered trademark in the European Union and other countries.

ISBN-13: 978–0–230–00134–3
ISBN-10: 0–230–00134–3

This book is printed on paper suitable for recycling and made from fully managed and sustained forest sources. Logging, pulping and manufacturing processes are expected to conform to the environmental regulations of the country of origin.

A catalogue record for this book is available from the British Library.

A catalog record for this book is available from the Library of Congress.

10 9 8 7 6 5 4 3 2 1
16 15 14 13 12 11 10 09 08 07

Printed and bound in China

Editors' Note
The chapters in the book reflect the viewpoints of the individuals. They were not written by the individuals but we used their own words from our verbal interviews.

CONTENTS

About the authors   7
Introduction   9

David Halberstam
Opening a window on the society   12

Edward Albee
Collecting ideas from the unconscious mind   24

Dale Chihuly
Exploiting controlled accidents   34

Daniel Libeskind
Creating reality with architecture   **44**

Nandan Nilekani
Visualizing the future of global business   56

Erica Jong
Seducing her own demons   64

Julie Taymor
Moving, touching, entertaining and inspiring people   74

James Rosenquist
Making an illusion on two-dimensional surfaces   84

Steve Wozniak
Inventing to simplify things   98

Roland Heiler
Overruling the tendency to compromise   108

Milton Glaser
Being a design generalist   120

Chuck Close
Decoding the mysterious process of art   *130*

Spike Lee
Changing the filmmaking landscape   *146*

Chris Bangle
Creating the personification of BMW Group design   *156*

Paul Warwick Thompson
Looking for enduring significance   *170*

Marvin Hamlisch
Composing and collaboration   *180*

Steven Holl
Breaking the rules   *186*

Ilana Goor
My best things are my mistakes   *200*

Ken Heyman
Seeing more than others see   *212*

Karim Rashid
Changing the aesthetics of product design   *224*

Acknowledgments   *236*

ABOUT THE AUTHORS

Herbert Meyers and Richard Gerstman are the retired founding partners of Gerstman+Meyers (now Interbrand), a global design consultancy. Their passion for creativity stems from guiding their company for 35 years during which the firm won over 300 design awards.

Herb Meyers was born in Germany and came to the United States in 1939. After serving as an interpreter in the United States Army Air Corps during World War II, he studied design at Pratt Institute from where he gained a Bachelor of Fine Arts.

Richard Gerstman graduated as an industrial designer from the University of Cincinnati, then worked in both Norway and Sweden, countries that were in the forefront of design at the time, before returning to the United States where he opened his own design studio.

In 1970, Herb Meyers and Richard Gerstman met and founded Gerstman+Meyers. Both realized early in their careers that design is an influential component of doing business and marketing goods. Starting as a small group, they initially did everything from designing to supervising, client contact, writing proposals and new business development.

As the business grew in reputation and number of clients, their firm pioneered unique design solutions based on market conditions and aesthetics. Together with their staff, they provided services in brand identity and package design, corporate identity, and environmental interiors for major corporations in the United States, Canada, South America, Europe and East Asia.

Actively pursuing their passion for creativity, Herb and Richard never relaxed their focus on building a reputation of professional excellence and reliability, while servicing a virtual who's who list of corporate clients such as Johnson & Johnson, Procter & Gamble, AT&T, Heinz, Kellogg's, Exxon, Ralston-Purina, General Motors, Pepsi-Cola and Omni Hotels.

To service their overseas clients, Global Design Network (GDN), a Gerstman+Meyers subsidiary in Canada, Europe and South America, was formed. Clients included BASF, Bayer AG, Boehringer Mannheim, Deutsche Telecom, Ciba, JTI (Japan), and Brahma (Brazil).

In 1996, Gerstman+Meyers became part of the Interbrand Group, one of the world's leading brand consultancies, from where Richard Gerstman retired in 2004 as chairman emeritus Interbrand US.

Both authors have been frequent writers and lecturers on subjects relating to creativity and design and recently co-authored the books *Branding @ the digital age* (2002) and *The Visionary Package* (2005), both published by Palgrave Macmillan. Herb Meyers also co-authored *The Marketer's Guide to Successful Package Design* (McGraw-Hill).

INTRODUCTION

"The creation of a thousand forests is in one acorn."
Ralph Waldo Emerson

Most of us grew up watching movies, reading books and, in some instances, enjoyed museums, concerts, art galleries, theater and dance, along with an appreciation of paintings, sculpture, architecture and product design. When we think of all the creative ventures that delight our senses, we often take for granted why they entertain.

These creative ventures did not just happen. They were conceived and they happened because someone created them so that other people would enjoy them. They wanted to express their ideas and stimulate their audience by a venture, and thereby create a movie, a play, a book, a car, a building or a service that they hoped would delight and be useful to their audience.

Hearing from creative people

There are books written about creations that have delighted us. Many books have been written about the creators themselves – describing their lives and their accomplishments.

For this book, we wanted to look at creativity from a different angle. We wanted to hear from creative people themselves and find out how they dream up their ideas and thoughts that others had never before envisaged. We wanted them to be the subjects of this book. We wanted their responses and their personal viewpoints, so that the readers of this book could understand how the creative people have been motivated, and how they have succeeded in influencing, and sometimes substantially changing, lifestyles and conditions that surround us on a daily basis.

With thousands of people around the world wanting to enter and excel in their creative fields, a relatively small percentage is successful in terms of fame. The creative people we interviewed for this book are all successful in their fields, and many are known around the world for their successful creative work.

Each chapter in the book represents a creative person expressing his or her views on creativity, their thinking process and the steps they take to create things that delight their audiences. Some describe their incentives and some describe the methods used for creating and solving problems that may arise along the way.

For the interest of our readers, we identified accomplished people from a wide range of professional activities: art, architecture, literature, design, stage and screen, music, theater and business. The interviewees range widely in age and countries of origin.

We felt that hearing from these successful creative people not only may help us to understand the steps to becoming successful in a creative field, but also may inspire some of our readers to follow a creative path.

Motivations for creativity

We often find that the creative venues such as museums, theaters, art galleries and concerts take place in the larger cities around the world. Does this mean that there's less exposure to creativity in small towns? Since we selected our interviewees on the basis of their fields and their accomplishments, we did not know in advance whether a small town or large city atmosphere was important to their upbringing and growth in their creative fields. We were surprised by many of the interview responses.

Their answers were illuminating, based upon their own backgrounds and experience. Most of them spoke about their influence from childhood in creative endeavors and what motivated them to look for new ideas and carry them through to influence the outside world. You will notice how the interviewees speak from their hearts and give their personal feelings about their work, their experiences and their audiences.

It is also interesting to hear from our interviewees what drove them to express their creativity. What were their personalities like? Were they influenced by their parents? Were the creative people loners? Did they start being creative early in life or at a later age?

We wanted to find the answers to these and many other questions. Can you learn to be creative? Can you make people creative who are not initially creative? What's the impetus to be creative? Is money an important motivation to creativity? Or is it fame? If neither, what drives creative people to do what they do?

These questions are answered by many of the interviewees who express a range of different and interesting viewpoints.

We found certain characteristics that were shared by these accomplished creative people. Common themes emerged – sharing the creative experience with others; breaking the rules; personal satisfaction; discovery and individualism – described differently by each.

Dreaming up ideas

There were substantial differences among the interviewees when expressing their views on how they come up with ideas. This is quite fascinating, because the crux of creativity is based on good ideas that are unique enough to stimulate the outside world.

The different viewpoints of these creative people will impress the readers of this book, and we believe readers will:

- be encouraged and stimulated by recognizing how the creative mind works
- understand how different creative people are motivated
- appreciate how different creative people solve problems in different ways
- find out how creative people have been inspired to create
- see how creativity influences the marketplace and our lifestyles
- recognize that creative lifestyles vary substantially
- realize how their early years have influenced their creative activities
- note how creative people tolerate criticism.

An enjoyable part of interviewing the creative people was visiting their homes, studios or offices to see where they worked and where they created. Each of these places expressed the personality of the artist – a very eclectic design studio, a vacation home, a city town house, a business office, a studio with architectural models, a museum, a painter's studio. Although the reader won't have the experience of physically meeting the interviewees in their place of creativity, we believe the physical presence of the person interviewed in the chapter is expressed through their narratives and the photographs throughout this book.

Many in the book expressed the view that the challenge for the future will be in our educational system and that if creativity is not encouraged in our educational system, the future for the creative arts will only thrive in those parts of the world where it is encouraged.

Our passion for writing this book was fueled by our creative backgrounds in the design profession. We found the interviews with these creative and successful individuals very exciting and stimulating and believe that the readers of this book will be equally encouraged and inspired by the personal viewpoints expressed in the book.

DAVID HALBERSTAM

Opening a window on the society

David Halberstam, one of the most distinguished social and political writers in America, has faithfully chronicled the profound changes in the second half of the twentieth century and the challenges of the twenty-first century. His writing career started as a newspaper reporter when he covered the beginnings of the American civil rights movement. Then, for his reporting on the Vietnam War for the New York Times, *he won a Pulitzer prize. He is well known for his influential and best-selling books that appeal to periods of American life, including* The Best and the Brightest, The Powers That Be, The Fifties, Playing for Keeps, The Reckoning *and* Summer of '49.

It is with deep regret that several months after our interview with David Halberstam, he was killed in an automobile accident. His important message in this book will remain a document of his contribution to great journalism.

Creativity is interesting because it's something that we do not explore and something we do not know much about.

I think a creative person is someone who is uncomfortable in the conventional setting and cannot really function well there. This is someone who cannot go to the office every day from nine to five. Someone who has to figure out things on his or her own and then set boundaries that are personal rather than institutional.

With creativity, there's a high level of individualism and you have to trust your instincts. You have a sixth sense of how to go about things, where your intellectual and emotional talents combine to give you a gift that other people don't have. Even as you are making choices, you don't realize that you're making choices – you don't know that your brain is clicking off what you do want and what you don't want. It's happening because you're thinking intuitively. It's about maximizing personal choice and personal freedom and knowing that you have some skill that's a little unusual. And you want to protect and maximize that skill.

I'm sure there are a lot of people who are very creative, but are not seeking

David Halberstam. *Photo: Frederick G.S. Clow*

creative work. Our best young college graduates, people who should probably be teaching in high school or college, writing or doing other things, are, for whatever reason, going to law school and business school. A lot of them are probably very creative, and I suspect that, down the road, a lot of them are going to be very unhappy, regretting the more conventional choices they've made.

I don't think money stirs creativity. I think that if you're naturally creative, you end up doing it because you cannot do anything else. When I went into journalism, it paid poorly and it was not particularly glamorous. But when you're creative, you do what you do, and it is not for the money. If you think "I want to be famous," or "I want to make a lot of money," my sense is that you don't go into most creative jobs.

> If you think "I want to be famous," or "I want to make a lot of money," my sense is that you don't go into most creative jobs.

A couple of years ago I gave a commencement speech at Dartmouth, and I said that the most important thing in life is to find out what it is you love the most and do it. If you choose something you love, you're likely to do it well. I recently visited *The Harvard Crimson* where I spent most of my college years and everybody there was going to be a consultant, not a journalist. They were going to be consultants because they could start at high salaries. And I said to them, "Did it ever strike you that the only reason why they pay you that much money is the fact that you would not take the job unless they paid you that much money? And that you may be passing on something that you really want and will miss out on?"

How I became a journalist

Several things influenced my writing ability. I knew I didn't want to go to law school, especially when I saw the size of the law school textbooks. And based on my marks, I was not going to be someone with a Ph.D. and teach in college. When you look at the grades that I had, and the attitudes that I had when I was young, most of my teachers would have been very surprised that I would do well.

My mother was a schoolteacher and my father was a doctor. Both were ardent readers. I remember one year, *My Weekly Reader* tried to hire my mother to take a job and leave her job teaching second grade. She thought about it, but she did not want to give up that three-month teachers' vacation. She depended on that.

When my father was overseas during World War II, we first lived in the Bronx, then in Winsted, Connecticut, then in El Paso and Austin, Texas, then briefly in Rochester, Minnesota – the Mayo Clinic – and then back to Winsted. At each place, the first thing my mother did was to march us to the library, and we would duly get our library cards and take out books. So obviously there was a background in which books were important.

I was easily bored as a kid – I had some kind of learning disorder – surely a minor one. But I was bored easily and quickly, and that often translated into marginal grades. Thinking back, I can still see myself in the fifth grade in Winsted, Connecticut, in effect flying out the window. If a course or a teacher didn't interest me, I just flew away. If I had a course that interested me, I would do very well, but I was not someone who could do well at all things.

Harvard was a lot easier in 1951 and I probably had good enough SATs in English and history to get in. Today, you would not get into Harvard with my marks. Oddly enough, I was good at math, which surprised me because I couldn't wait to get away from math. I did well in math as long as it made sense, but when we got to trigonometry, for example, I thought those numbers had no meaning nor any truth.

While at Harvard, I was managing editor of *The Harvard Crimson*. It was a very good paper. We had Tony Lukas, also a Pulitzer prizewinner, along with others who became distinguished authors. *The Crimson* was a hot place at the time and if you were managing *The Crimson*, you had done well in a competition with your colleagues.

I was good at it and I was very quick. It was clearly the only thing that I had ever been good at. I was not good in the more traditional things. I remember that the career choices were rather narrow then – it really was doctor, lawyer, Wall Street. People did not think about going to Hollywood, or writing for *The National Lampoon*, or going to work as writers for *Saturday Night Live*. I wasn't going to go to Wall Street or into the CIA. Nor was I going to be an academic or a lawyer.

The normal career choices were blocked for me, since they were not things I thought I could do. I think when you've got a learning disability, you have a lot of hope, ambition, optimism, but you also see all these other routes that are blocked – things that are too hard for you. You are not going to go there, or if you do go there, you are going to be unhappy and always a little bit out of synch. But when you see one place where the door is open – where you feel your skills are applicable – you go for it and you work harder than anyone else.

> ... when you see one place where the door is open you go for it and you work harder than anyone else.

On *The Harvard Crimson* I was very good at being a journalist, because it was auditory work and you got answers by asking questions – it didn't come from books. My friends on the paper were Magnas and Summas, and they got Rhodes and Fulbright scholarships. I was in the bottom half of my class – possibly the bottom third. Nevertheless, I just got elected, this past year, as an honorary member of Phi Beta Kappa. This is a great joke in the family since it took me fifty years to get there.

Academically, I graduated without honors, and my first job was as the one reporter on a small daily in Mississippi in 1955. The moment I got there, I took off in a career sense, because I was learning auditory, I was thinking and I was connecting events to real people.

Once I applied my intelligence to what was around me – the politics and the daily life of the community – once I could make reads on the people I was interviewing, getting them right, who and what they were, judging them, figuring them out, I self-evidently had a talent. I was free from the world of academics and I began to take off and could go out to where the world was real. I found that I had a natural ability to get a sense of who people were and what they were *not* saying.

> When people in the creative process get their hands on what they love, they are ferocious ... because they have a sense of how few other options there are.

It was clear by then what I was going to do, because I loved journalism and was good at it. But I don't think you go into it for riches or money. I can't speak for music, art or whatever. But if you go into journalism, you go out of love, out of ego, out of who you are, and not wanting to do other things. Other things look to you like prisons and you're terrified of the boredom.

I would not have been very good in a large corporation, since I was not someone who was going to be good at taking orders. I knew that journalism was the only ticket I could get and therefore I was going to maximize it. I decided that no one was going to work harder.

Doing the one thing you do well is important in the creative process. You want to do things that you know you are good at and that you are not going to get a lot of chances to do them.

I think that's probably true of a lot of creative people. For them, creativity is often an all or nothing thing. When people in the creative process get their hands on what they love, they are ferocious, not just because they are doing something they love but because they have a sense of how few other options there are. In effect, it's *succeed handsomely at this one thing or fail miserably at everything else*.

When I did well for the *New York Times*, it was overseas, away from the office atmosphere. Even a place like the *New York Times* has an office, whether it's in New York or Washington. Those are bureaus and you have to take assignments, whereas in the three assignments I had overseas – Leopoldville, capital of Congo, Vietnam and, eventually, Eastern Europe – I was the bureau chief. In effect I was my own managing editor, and I was my own assignment editor. I could make up my own stories and do what I wanted. No one was telling me what to do. No one ever assigned me a story. I did it all myself. It was wonderful for me. I think that one of the reasons I flowered there was because I was not in someone else's bureau.

I could not operate if someone said to me, "We would like you to do a book on industrial development in Japan and Detroit, and it will take four or five years," I probably would have resented it. But if I stumbled on it myself, I may think, "Hmm, that's interesting and maybe I can do that," then it might work out just fine. A lot of it is your own emotional attitude. In an office, I'd be restless and in conflict with people, but outside an office, I think I'm really good as a colleague.

I wanted the excitement of journalism without boredom. I didn't want to do anything by rote, by repetition. It was a lucky choice for me – I was paid to learn and I could go out and talk to people and it was going to be different every day.

My early successes

Exactly fifty years ago, within two months of graduating from college, my first article was published in a national magazine. It was a magazine called *The Reporter*, which was a sophisticated biweekly with good art. I did four pieces for them in that first year.

I was fortunate to have a very blessed life and exciting projects. After working at a small daily paper in Mississippi, I worked for four years at a wonderful paper in Nashville, Tennessee. Starting early on in the civil rights movement, I wrote about the Emmet Till trial in 1955. Then in November 1960, when I was twenty-six, I joined the *New York Times*. It was the day after John Kennedy's election. Within a couple of months I was in the Congo with a big story, since it was an early military political conflict.

> Very early on in Vietnam, I realized that I was not only covering a very big story but that I was involuntarily at the epicenter of a great collision between the American government and the American press.

Then, when I was twenty-eight, I volunteered for Vietnam in its very early days. I thought it was going to be a big story, and I had learned how, in the Congo, to deal with what I call "the fear thing" or being in combat. I was young and single, so I thought I would do it and that it was worth the risk.

Very early on in Vietnam, I realized that I was not only covering a very big story but that I was involuntarily at the epicenter of a great collision between the American government and the American press. Because it didn't work. Not from the start. The premise of the policy was false. The government was telling a bunch of lies about how well we were doing, when it was obvious that we were failing.

If you are the *New York Times* reporter at a moment when there is a war going on, and the government of the United States and a variety of political leaders are lying, you become the reporter for the most powerful journalistic instrument in the country. You're charged with telling the truth, and that means that you're in for one hell of a collision with the government, with the right wing, with the military, and with the Defense Department. It was a very edgy painful time – much of the criticism was extremely painful.

President Kennedy asked the publisher of the *New York Times* to pull me out of there. The Defense Department went after me and after my sources, trying to find out if I was a Communist. It was very ugly stuff – constant attacks on my patriotism and my manhood. It caught me completely by surprise. I thought all I had to do was cover a war, take the allotted number of risks and get it right. I didn't realize that the more I got it right, the more my own government would turn on me.

> I didn't realize that the more I got it right, the more my own government would turn on me.

It's different today. Nobody is surprised any longer when a bunch of reporters say the government is not telling the truth. We're much better prepared for it. I kept saying before we went into Iraq that we were punching our fist into the largest hornet's nest in the world. The people who thought we should go into Baghdad had been watching the movie *Patton* too often. They should have been watching *The Battle of Algiers* by Gillo Pontecorvo, the great movie on the French Algerian war and the urban insurgency against the French.

But the Vietnam experience was extraordinary and if you are a reporter, you know that it's only going to happen once. You can't sit there waiting for that to happen, and so you go on with your life and write books.

The books I like to write

There are two kinds of books that I have been writing. The first are serious books that reflect important challenges and historical moments in the country. These books reflect a lot about our society – whether it is about race, the coming of television, or the changes in authority. I'll be coming out soon with a book on the Chinese entering the war in Korea, which I've been working on for four years.

And then there are my sports books, which are great fun. I've somehow ended up writing seven of them and they give me a wonderful change of pace. Actually, those seven books are not just about sports. They're a reflection on the changing values on our society in America, caused by television, by big money,

Moishe Tshombe, president of Katanga province in the Congo, is describing the capture of an Irish UN contingent of about 100 members by his white mercenary army. During the Congo turmoil in 1961, David Halberstam (in sunglasses) was a 27-year-old correspondent for the *New York Times*. *Collection of David Halberstam*

and the impact of all that on a small theater called athletics. Sports are a great window on the society. You can learn a lot about America that way.

When you write books, you pick what interests you creatively and has societal value. You don't want to write for four years about Korea if it's not interesting to you and if it doesn't have some larger truth for the society. The tests are: Will you be able to sustain your curiosity for four years, and will it have larger meaning? These are important questions, and if the answers are affirmative, the assumption is that enough of your fellow citizens will want to buy the book. Then you can go ahead.

> Sports are a great
> window on the society.

The young Vietnam War correspondents in 1963. *Left to right:* David Halberstam, Malcolm W. Browne and Niel Sheehan. *Collection of David Halberstam*

You are always searching and thinking, "What's going on in America? How do you portray it? What are the forces at play? What is in conflict? What do you need to know? What are the changes?" You are always auditioning ideas and looking for something that will interest you.

I remember doing *The Reckoning*, which was about Japan, the auto industry and the decline of Detroit. I thought, "How could this have happened?" I was a child of that time in World War II when you had the cover of *Life* and had airplanes and Jeeps as far as the eye could see in Detroit. America was the great industrial power, and had come to the zenith of its power by the end of World War II, and Japan had been reduced to ashes.

And here was Japan, taking something that had always been an American signature, the making of an automobile, and doing it better than we were. What made Japan rise from the ashes, and what was it about America that had let us become so careless? It was obviously something that affected who we were as a society.

I didn't want it to be a business book, but an attempt to define who we are and what had happened to us in the years since World War II. I had to understand the auto industry and why it had become strong over there and why it had softened here. I decided to take a Japanese and an American company – Nissan and Ford – side by side.

> You are always searching and thinking, "What's going on in America? How do you portray it? What are the forces at play? What is in conflict? What do you need to know? What are the changes?"

Detroit is not an easy place to work. But Japan is a *very*, *very* difficult place to work, not so much because of the language, but because of the cultural inhibitions. The difficulty was not getting stuff translated from an interview, but the wariness of the Japanese to be forthcoming, because they have been taught all their lives not to call attention to themselves.

But once I had the idea, I thought it was a very valuable one. I'm not a business reporter, but I needed to have an inside knowledge of business. It took six years and I learned a hell of a lot.

It was a very difficult book for me. It was like retooling myself and going to a graduate school again for five or six years. But, in a way, I think it's my most skillful book because it's a hard subject to make interesting. Industrial decline is not a sexy subject. Cars themselves are sexy for their hot new style, not for the decline of the car-making process. I was proud of the result and I felt I had grown an additional notch intellectually.

You look for an idea that is right for you with a larger truth about the society in it. And that's generally been my approach, telling something that helps explain who we are to our fellow Americans.

I doubt that many of my traditional readers stayed with me on that book. They wanted something more political, or more sociological. Nevertheless, the book did very well, but with a slightly different constituency.

As an author, you and the reader have a partnership. The reader comes in and he or she thinks, "Okay, I've read a couple of books by him before, and he's pretty straight, and he works hard and he does the requisite legwork. So I'll buy this book because, generally, his books are accessible and he makes it more fun than most to read." And they read it.

But with whom they are, their prejudices, their generational age and something they thought they understood and then added more dimension to it, there's no guarantee that they will take the exact same lessons from me that I think I'm putting out. What you say and what they hear are often very different things.

The book I did on *The Fifties* was an attempt to explain a decade that everybody thought was a very quiescent and boring decade. I tried to show how all the stuff that took place in the 1960s had really evolved from the 1950s.

You look for an idea that is right for you with a larger truth about the society in it.

By the time I did it, we had all lived through the 1960s and 1970s. The roots of Vietnam were in it, along with the McCarthy episode and the rise of television. There had been this explosion of sexual change and the revolution from the pill. And the changes and challenges with civil rights manifested in the 1960s. It began in the fifties with *Brown* v. *Board of Education*. I thought a book that traced the 1960s back to the 1950s would be of value. My friend Murray Kempton used to say that one of my strengths was that I like to take things, find out how they work, and explain them. And that's not a bad thing to have said about you.

When you start a book, you don't know exactly where you're going with it. It's a journey, and you look and think, "Well, it's going to go this way," and then it goes another way.

A book has an orbital thrust all its own. You want it to answer questions that challenge you. You want the answers to be interesting to you and to a broad base of readers. You know that once you start, you're going to go in many different directions that you could not have predicted.

My work and my influence

I think it's presumptive to think that my books have influenced society. You put them out there, and in this very complicated, pluralistic society where there are so many different voices, they either become part of something larger or they don't. They may or may not become part of a changed attitude on how we perceive these things.

If you are coming out with a book once every four years, do you really have any influence? Maybe people who are in government, who are not too ideological, read these books and they become a part of the larger debate. I think that some of the stuff I did on Vietnam was part of a larger debate. And that is all the influence you can hope for.

A book has an orbital thrust all its own.

I was very uneasy with journalists I knew back in the 1960s who specifically wrote as if they were trying to change the minds of people in Washington, wanting so badly to be major players. You write based on your sense of truth and your interests. If you do that well, and it has this ancillary effect and it becomes part of the debate, fine. But you don't set out to be a part of the debate or to be a big time player.

The Best and the Brightest probably did bring skepticism toward government officials who blandly announce, "We're doing this and this and it's good for you." In my book, there is that skepticism, as well there should be.

I think any writer or any historian working in this era would do well to be modest about the influence of his or her books. It's a country of 300 million, a communication society, an entertainment society and a disposable society. The staying power of any book is infinitely more limited than it was thirty years ago. A book comes out today, and it is enormously important for about six days, but because we are so volatile, the society quickly turns its attention to something else.

> You know that once you start, you're going to go in many different directions that you could not have predicted.

The subjects I've chosen for my books have been interesting and the books have done well. The new book will be my twenty-first. The real gift is not to be bored doing it. If the books sell well and your constituents keep buying them and you remain independent, that is a great gift – a privileged life.

I'm content to think that, for fifty years, I've done what I love. I'm happy to have been handsomely rewarded in terms of societal honors and I've been able to have a very nice standard of income and, most importantly, a great deal of creative independence.

If I were drawing up a life fifty years ago when I graduated from college, I wouldn't have dared to draw up a life like this. It would have been beyond reach!

EDWARD ALBEE

Collecting ideas from the unconscious mind

Edward Albee, the American playwright, is known for works and themes that have changed the landscape of American drama. His well-known plays – such as Who's Afraid of Virginia Woolf? The Zoo Story, Three Tall Women *and* The Sandbox *– are often complex examinations of the modern condition. The originality he continues to bring to his productions makes him distinct from other playwrights of his era. He has received three Pulitzer prizes, a Tony Award for Lifetime Achievement, the National Medal of Arts and other honors. He frequently speaks at university campuses and is president of the Edward F. Albee Foundation, which maintains a writers' and artists' colony.*

T he most important thing about creativity, and the making of art, is that we are the only animal that does it. We are the animal that has invented metaphor. We create art to render consciousness comprehensible. In that sense, we are the only creative animal and this is what distinguishes us fundamentally. I'm convinced that creativity is determined by some quirk in the neurological pathways of our brain.

Many people in the world have the same experiences, depending upon their intelligence, their sensitivity, and their willingness to pay attention to what is going on.

The only thing that separates the creative from the non-creative is the fact that creative people are not content merely to have the experience, but insist on commenting on it.

> The only thing that separates the creative from the non-creative is the fact that creative people are not content merely to have the experience, but insist on commenting on it.

Some people translate these experiences into something such as paintings, plays or classical music. Art is the comment they make on the experience that everybody else has had. The very best do it because they are incomplete without doing it.

Children, very young, tend to be infinitely, naturally creative. We see wonderful paintings and drawings by four-, five- and six-year-old kids – but that creativity most often goes away.

Edward Albee. *Photo: Jerry Speier*

And something else goes away too. When very young, a lot of people can see color in sounds – they hear a sound and they realize that's a green sound or a blue sound. It's that interesting creative transference that takes place naturally in young people. A lot of young kids have this but it goes away completely. I experienced that myself when I was quite young, and I've since read up a lot about it. Unfortunately, many families drive it out of young people.

But those of us who respond very young to music, for example, or painting, or literature, as I did, stand a chance of our creativity not going away, and we can use it as we grow up. We can have all these responses, but without the strange neurological stuff in our brain, we're not likely to use them.

My creative youth

I had very, very young responses. I started doing drawings when I was six. I heard my first Bach and Mozart when I was eight or nine and started listening to music. I have always read beyond my years, and I started writing poetry when I was nine and just kept right on going.

I wrote poetry for twenty years and stopped because I was not getting much better – just a little better. I wrote two novels in my teens. Nobody could write worse novels in their teens than the two I wrote. I was bad at short stories. I didn't hit on playwriting until I was twenty-eight. The instant that I wrote *The Zoo Story*, my first play, I realized that this is what I should be doing. It felt natural to me. And that turned out to be right.

> Too many families and schools discourage creativity. I left home because I was determined to do what I wanted to do.

But everybody is different creatively. I think everybody finds what he or she is going to be at different ages. Mozart was a great composer when he was five years old. Bernard Shaw didn't write his first play until he was over forty. Rossini stopped composing when he was twenty-nine. Everybody is different for all sorts of reasons.

Good music and reading turned me more and more into the kind of person who was going to be able, when the time came, to comment and make that transition from the experience to the useful exploitation of the experience.

What started me drawing? I saw drawings and I thought that would be interesting. I started writing because I was reading a lot and I thought that would be interesting.

My parents were mildly appalled – these were my adoptive parents. We didn't get along and I left home when I was eighteen because everything I wanted to do was completely the opposite of everything they wanted me to do. So I just left. I couldn't take it anymore. Too many families and schools

Playwrights Unit, c.1965. Left to right: Edward Albee, Lanford Wilson, Paul Foster, Kenneth Pressman, Lawrence Osgood, Adrienne Kennedy, Lee Kalcheim. *Alix Jeffrey Photograph Archive, The Harvard Theater Collection, Houghton Library*

discourage creativity. I left home because I was determined to do what I wanted to do.

I had been writing for a long time – not very well – but I was getting published in school literary magazines. I had two poems published in tiny West Texas poetry magazines when I was sixteen. I was getting known, but my stuff wasn't very good until I started writing plays.

There were many influences – many great artists and everything I read and looked at. When I was thirteen, I was reading Ivan Turgenev, which is not even natural for Russians to be reading. But I was reading all Turgenev's novels and people like that. So I was reading beyond my years, and listening beyond my years, and always looking beyond my years.

My school education was first at home and then away at Lawrenceville and Choate. I had very good teachers who seemed to sense that I had something odd about me. They pushed me toward experiencing the arts. They steered me away from the junk to the good stuff. They saw that I liked to draw, so they showed me good art. All this was very helpful.

My thoughts about education today

Although the arts were not especially encouraged nationwide when I went to school, it was better than what goes on in schools in America today, where there's no art education at all. It's shocking and disgusting.

In schools today, the only goal is getting a good job and making a lot of money. That's apparently the only goal of American culture these days and it's worse than sad. It's destructive. America will never be a great society or great civilization without a decent educational system. We do not have one right now and it's getting worse all the time.

> The great majority of the senators and representatives who I've talked to over the years are fearful of the arts.

The entering class at Harvard University a few years ago was asked, "Why do you want to be at Harvard?" Seventy percent of the kids who replied said, "So that when I graduate I'll be able to get a high-paying job." Is that a good reason to be educated?

I think that most of the people who think, "Gee, it would be good to be a film writer because you make a lot of money that way," are going to be as lousy as most of today's film writers are. I think the need to create doesn't have anything to do with money. If you can make money by it, that's nice, but if that's your only goal, you're not going to be a very good artist.

I admire most creative people as long as they are serious about their art and are not in it just for money or fame. Money and fame are two highly destructive things to creative artists. A lot of careers are destroyed by the emphasis on making money and being highly commercial. You can be rotten and still have that need. Or, if you want to be very, very good, you do it because it is your nature to do it, and not just because you're going to make a buck out of it.

Creative people can be discouraged if they perceive that they're not going to make a good living. Unfortunately, in America today, unless you're making a lot of money you're considered to be a Democrat or something even worse.

I've gone down to Washington and spent a lot of time talking to senators and representatives to plead for the arts and the National Endowment and various charitable organizations for the arts. I'm startled by the fear and loathing that so many of our representatives have for the arts. The great majority of the senators and representatives who I've talked to over the years are fearful of the arts. They see people in the arts as corrupt and destructive liberals. It stands to reason that I've never met a decent creative artist who was a Republican.

I think these people in our government are fearful of the arts because the arts educate us in how to think about living our lives, how to participate in a democracy and how to vote intelligently – and that this may lead to a different kind of government than the majority of these people want.

Of course, there are an awful lot of people in business who are deeply involved in supporting the arts, and we're grateful for them. It could be that those are people who wish that they were creative artists themselves.

The good and the bad creative artists

With creative people, there are good and bad ones, there are useful and useless ones. And being educated is to know the difference.

There probably have been a lot of potential composers, and painters, and poets, and novelists who have never written anything and never will. Perhaps most of them would be terrible, anyway. Since one out of every hundred things that occur in the arts is any good, and 99 percent of them are bad, it is probably just as well that they didn't happen. Or if they did happen, they should be dismissed. Most art is awful. Terrible. And that includes a lot of very popular stuff. So if you want to encourage more people to perform in the arts, maybe one out of a hundred of them will do something useful.

You cannot invent that which is not there. What you can do is persuade people to participate in the arts more fully. To experience it more and learn more from it. But that won't necessarily make them creative. You can't make people creative who are not creative.

People can be encouraged to be creative only if they are stimulated by what they've experienced and not only by what is popular. The ability to absorb what happens to you and to learn from it is something that you have to maintain within yourself. It's not something that is built in.

In the same way, I cannot teach anybody how to be a playwright. I can teach somebody how to write plays the way other people did, but I cannot make anybody who is not a playwright into a playwright. I can only help somebody who is a playwright to practice the craft better.

> … that's my creative process, getting access to what the unconscious has been doing and helping it to move consciously.

Where my ideas come from

A playwright needs ideas, and here's the part of creativity that nobody wants to talk about – where ideas come from. I believe they come from the unconscious. As for me, I don't look for ideas, but ideas look for me.

There are some writers who are didactic, who say, "Now I must find a subject that is going to be sociologically interesting, or psychologically interesting." Then they get an idea – they invent something, or steal something from somebody else and find people who can populate the idea. The whole thing is a kind of a construction. It's didactic and fairly tedious.

I discover one day that I have been thinking about a play. I have been thinking about it in the unconscious mind for a long time. And all of a sudden, it is moving to the conscious mind. And so that's my creative process, getting access

Edward Albee (left) at his Montauk house with his producer, Richard Barr, and unidentified woman, c.1975.
Courtesy of the Edward Albee Collection. Photo: Jay Hoops

to what the unconscious has been doing and helping it to move consciously. That's how it works for me, and I don't fuss with it.

The thinking process is intuitive to a great part. Two things are going on. I am convinced that the intuitive development of a piece happens mostly in the unconscious mind. But the control – the aesthetic and thematic control of how you make this dramatically effective – that demands an awful lot of *conscious* work. So the *unconscious* and the *conscious* are both working feverishly together in a thing like this.

I very seldom know what generates a play in my head. Because obviously, whatever it is has sunk into the unconscious, which is far more organized than my conscious mind. I've been told that about 90 percent of mental activity occurs in the unconscious, so I rely upon it to do its job. And I don't interfere with it.

I let ideas fester a long time before I put them down on paper. Six months, two years. I let them develop while I do something else. They seem to want to do it that way.

I certainly don't block or frame out the work. Doing that is such a limitation. Some do, and they are mostly didactic writers. I start at the beginning and go to the end. Because if you block out what you are allowing yourself to do, and then something more interesting comes along, you don't do it.

Very few of my plays rely on past experiences. Why limit yourself to only what you have experienced? Why do a thing like that? Why not invent characters as part of the creative act? The particulars can alter, of course, the more I get to know about the characters and the situations.

And I don't write things down until I'm really ready to write them down. I become aware of something. I've been thinking about this, and it's interesting. I may not think about it again for another year. The next time I think about it, it could be further along, or it may have gone away. Usually it's further along. And so I let it develop as it wants to develop. I wait until the play wants to be written down and *then* I write it down. To my memory, I've never started a piece that I didn't finish.

But everybody has a different way of doing this. The important thing is to let the unconscious have its head, so to speak. Let it do most of the work and most of the development for you. Do not impose on it, and do not limit what the unconscious wants to do.

An idea is original with me. Whether it's original with anybody else is another matter. It doesn't concern me. Who said there are nine or eleven ideas or possible themes for a play? Somebody could be doing the same thing differently.

There's one thing I do know, that the play must have dramatic action. You can't write a perfectly good play about boring people sitting around with nothing happening to them, although that's what most of Broadway plays seem to me to be about. You must not let this happen. There must be interesting people and interesting things must be happening to them. Fortunately, those are the ideas that I get.

As I said, everything we write has been determined totally in the unconscious and we are merely putting it down on paper. Sometimes we get surprises, because we don't have good access to the unconscious. But unexpected surprises often upset people. That's why serious work is not as popular as junk. Junk is the same old stuff over and over again. People find it familiar and therefore comfortable.

How theater has changed

Unfortunately, theater has changed for the worse in the past few years. The dead hand of commerce has gotten in there a lot more. People are unwilling to take the chance they used to take on serious art – serious plays. They prefer what will make money, rather than what *should* be produced.

There are still a few people around who think theater is there because it is a serious art form and that we have to do serious work even though we may lose our shirts doing it. Some people still do that.

But the majority of the time, people are in it just as they are in it with movies. It is far easier to get financing for a $100 million movie than it is for a $2 million movie, because the $2 million movie is not going make a lot of money, and the $100 million movie can make $300–400 million. The whole state of mind these days is commerce.

The large productions often make the money, and what keeps destroying our culture is the assumption that what makes money is the best. Best-selling novels are never as good as the ones that do not sell as well. The most popular plays usually are nowhere near as good as the ones that don't run a long time.

More and more each year, the costs of producing and the expectation of the audience is dumbing down our theater audience the same as it's dumbing down the rest of our audiences.

Yet, some really great plays are produced, even though it's anticipated they might lose money. But for the most part it's very hard to get serious work produced. And serious work never runs as long as the junk does. Never. That is because of our education structure.

> ... many of my plays are about people missing the boat – getting to the end of their lives and realizing they have not fully lived them.

I'm more protective of my plays that have *not* been popular. I have twenty-eight plays now. There may be eight or nine of these that, I am sure, are going to have a perfectly good shelf life, and people are going to keep seeing and talking about them, because popularity produces more popularity. Every time *Who's Afraid of Virginia Woolf?* is done, somebody else does another production. But I have other plays, maybe eighteen or twenty of them, that do not get done as frequently as they should, even though I know that they are just as good, if not better than the more popular plays.

Why I like to write

All the same, I love being a playwright more than anything. And since I write longhand, I can work anywhere – in airplanes, on boats – anywhere. I get a lot of work done at my home in Montauk. Looking out at the ocean is very instructive and maybe that's why half of my plays are set outdoors.

For a vocation, I can't think of anything that I do that does not involve being a writer. I play less tennis than I used to. I don't fish. Swimming is exercise. But most of my life is spent with my eyes and ears open, which a writer must do. And I look at art, and I read books, and I listen to music. All these things are involved with keeping myself alert. The good playwrights who I know can write good plays, but they don't do other writing as well.

Some people write and tell me they have been influenced by my plays. A lot of writers tell me they have been influenced also. It is nice to make contact with people and if you can be helpful and useful – that is great.

I would like to influence their behavior, too. So many of my plays are about people missing the boat – getting to the end of their lives and realizing they have not fully lived them. I would like to persuade people to live their entire lives fully and dangerously, and

Edward Albee at his Montauk, NY home 2006.
Photo: Richard Gerstman

not just relax into getting through life. I find that terribly like death in life.

My fervent hope is that my plays have succeeded in influencing people to keep them awake – intellectually, emotionally and psycho- logically awake.

People who are willing to be influenced and examine the dilemmas that I put forward in my plays may learn something from them. Those people who think that they are perfect will learn nothing from my plays. And there is not much I can do about that.

As I said at the very beginning, creativity is a form of black magic and we cannot control it except to destroy it. I have observed the way ideas move from my unconscious to my conscious mind, and I think that leads me to the source of creativity, which is the unconscious. Talking about it too much might make it go away, so I am leery to talk about it and I don't like to talk very much about myself anyway.

I hope to continue being busy with my writing for many more years. I would really like to keep getting better as a writer as I go on. If I have enough sense to realize that I'm not writing well anymore, I hope I'll have enough sense to stop. And I consider all the arts to be fundamentally useful – not merely decorative. Decorative art is not enough. If what I do cannot be socially, politically, sociologically and psychologically useful, then there's no point in doing it. I hope I'll have enough good judgment to stop at that time.

DALE CHIHULY

Exploiting controlled accidents

Dale Chihuly, a prolific glass artist, is primarily lauded for moving blown glass out of the confines of small, precious objects and into the realm of large-scale contemporary sculpture. He is known for such memorable installation exhibitions as "Chihuly Over Venice" (1995–96), "Chihuly in the Light of Jerusalem 2000" and "Chihuly in the Park: A Garden of Glass" at Chicago's Garfield Park Conservatory (2001–02). This prodigious artist employs collaborative teams and a division of labor as part of the developmental process. He creates complex, multipart sculptures of dramatic beauty that place him in the forefront of the movement toward establishing the blown glass form as an accepted vehicle for installation and environmental arts.

For many people, being creative means having a lot of extra energy. A lot of people don't have a lot of energy, but I think artists generally do. And if you have the energy, what are you going to do with it? You can watch TV, or read a book, or go to the movies, or you can use your extra energy productively and do something creative. A lot of the artists I know fall into that category of having the energy to see what they can do with their energy.

How I came to be an artist

I always had a lot of energy and always wanted to put it to work somehow, even at early age. As a young man, I used it to draw a lot. I just wish that my mother had kept some of the drawings I did. She saw that I liked to draw, and she encouraged me to keep it up. Unfortunately, she never saved any of my drawings.

I was always interested in doing creative things. I started as someone who wanted to be an interior designer. But when I got out of college, I got a job that included weaving bits of glass into tapestries. This got me very interested in working with glass and so I set up my own little glass shop.

One night I melted some glass between four bricks. I didn't have a regular glassblowing pipe at that time, but I had a piece of some kind of scrap and I dipped it into the melted glass and blew a bubble. From that point on, I knew that I wanted to be a glassblower.

Dale Chihuly. *Photo: Bryan Ohno*

With that in mind, I enrolled in the hot glassblowing program of the University of Wisconsin, the first school to offer a glassblowing program. Then I took a course in ceramics at the Rhode Island School of Design and made several trips to Venice, the hub of the glassblowing industry at that time.

In 1971, I went out to the Pacific northwest and founded, together with some friends of mine, the Pilchuck Glass School in Stanwood, Washington, near Seattle, and set up my own studio in 1980.

How I work

As I said, I have always felt that, for me, creativity was really using excess energy. This has its ups and downs. To be truthful, when I don't feel well, I can't do much. But when I'm feeling good and exuberant and wanting to work, that's when I'm most creative.

You often read about some famous artists who had their blue period, and some of their work reflects that that was how they were feeling at the particular time when they produced that work. I always wondered how true that is. I have often wanted to do a little study by talking to authors who have written about such artists.

> ... I have always felt that, for me, creativity was really using excess energy.

Take van Gogh, for instance. He was depressed on and off and he only worked for nine years, and the last two or three were his most productive. I remember a van Gogh show a few years ago at the Metropolitan Museum in New York, called "Van Gogh in Arles," and it showed every painting he made while living in Arles, all in the right order. The show also included some of the letters that he sent to his brother, discussing his paintings. And when I looked at them, I tried to figure out at what point he felt great about what he was painting and at what point he was brooding. I'll tell you, I couldn't tell by looking at the paintings. They *all* looked great to me. I am sure he worked when he felt well, and also when he felt depressed, which was often. In either state, he didn't stop working.

So what I like to do is whatever it might take to feel good. But, whether or not I feel good, I'm fortunate that I have other great artists to work with. I have a big group of people, and we do all sorts of projects together. So if I occasionally feel a little down, I have other people around me who can carry the ball in terms of what we have to get done that day or that week. It's hard for me not to be there when I am the head of a project. I have to snap out of it if I'm not feeling creative. Often, if I'm not feeling very creative, I will work anyway. Then, when I later consider the fact that I didn't feel my best, I find that I did pretty

Yellow Boat, 2006, New York Botanical Garden, Bronx, New York. *Photo: Herb Meyers*

good work all the same. Like van Gogh, my work does not correspond with how I felt when I did it. And the reason that I get to notice that mood swings don't affect my work is that we have a lot of DVDs on my work and about different projects that I can review.

Many people ask me where my ideas come from. You never know where an idea comes from. Sometimes an idea just comes from the gut. You never know how it comes out – it just sort of happens.

Some of my ideas come directly from something I've seen. For instance, I did a series called *Pilchuck Baskets* that were directly influenced by seeing northwest coast Indian baskets. Another series that came after that are called *Seaforms*. They actually were an extension of the *Baskets* project. I blew them in a mold that, at a certain point, made them ribbed so that they looked like seashells, even though I wasn't really looking at any seashells at all. I just used that as a point of departure to start a new series. It was one of those things that just happen.

> You never know where an idea comes from. Sometimes an idea just comes from the gut.

Sometimes I'll be developing one series, and start to make changes on it in order to have something new happening. I usually have an idea that I think might have some possibilities and I'll go and do some experimenting. Half the time it leads to something that I can keep working on. Other times I give it up before the day is over because I just don't like what is going on.

I always felt that traveling gives me ideas, although I never made a series

Chihuly in the hot shop. *Photo: Russell Johnson*

named after a place, like *Arizona* or *Ireland*. But I did do a series that made me *think* of a place, a series called *Jerusalem Cylinders*. We also did a series called *Ulysses Cylinders*. But it's unusual for me to base an idea on a specific location. More likely, I may start with an idea and continue on it until it changes into something else.

A lot of the work just happens because I am experimenting. In other words, something might happen from what starts as one idea but may end up as something entirely different, something I didn't expect.

In glassblowing that works very well, because it's very tricky working with glass, and you can easily make a mistake and get something you weren't trying to get. If you are lucky, that can turn out to be good. What may start as an accident sometimes becomes a valuable exercise and, by trying it over and over, can turn into something that you can control. So you might say that a lot of our work is the result of sort of *controlled accidents*.

The hardest, and maybe the most enjoyable, part of being a creative person is making creative decisions. How long should you work on something before you decide whether it is worthwhile? And when do you abandon an idea and get on to something that is more promising? I think that's one of the things that make an artist an artist.

I have seen people work on ideas half their life that I could see would never be any good. The creative person really has to be the one who knows when to continue, and when to abandon an idea and to start something new. It's hard to explain how to control this type of decision making, but to be creative you have to have that ability. I'm not sure whether this applies to all creative fields – I have often wondered whether that would also apply to composing music, or writing a song, or if you are an author of novels.

Sometimes I get ideas from things I collect. I collect a lot of things – northwest coast Indian baskets, Pendleton blankets, wooden canoes, Curtis prints – and I have a collection of 300 accordions. I also collect old bird houses and remake them out of really good materials, which they weren't originally made from. I throw the old ones away, and put the new ones outside.

I used to collect cars, although I'm not collecting them any more. There was a cute little piece in the *New York Times* a few months ago. The *Times* called me and said, "Can we take a photograph of your Aston Martin?" I said, "Well, I don't have any more Aston Martins but I have an Austin Healey." I figured that's probably not what they wanted. But they said, "Great, we'd love to shoot the Austin Healey." A few days later, a guy comes and spends the entire day taking a frontal shot of my 1956 Austin Healey. And about three weeks later, there it was on the back cover of their design magazine. But all they showed was the grille of my Austin Healey with the caption "Dale Chihuly can't pass up a beautiful grille."

Anyway, some of the things I collect give me ideas that I may not otherwise have. It's just one of those things that work well for me.

Artists who influenced me

A few artists have influenced my work, but it's hard to name them. I mentioned one for you already, van Gogh. Andy Warhol was a big influence on me. He was alive when I was younger and I once traded with him. He wanted one of the pieces in my gallery and I was glad to do it. He has done so many things and influenced many creative people. He did a lot of movies that most people haven't seen. Many of them are pretty boring, but I still think they had a huge influence on filmmakers. And then he did *Interview* magazine, which was very avant-garde at the time it came out. It influenced magazines a great deal. He also had a band, a really hip band, before there were very many like it. He wrote a couple of books, designed shoes and even did store windows. I just find his work very interesting and it has made a lasting impression on me.

Also, Christo and Jeanne-Claude are among the artists who inspired me the most. I really connect with their projects and they way they do them. Some time ago, I saw a documentary film about one of their first big projects, called Valley Curtain at Rifle Gap in Colorado. The concept seemed like such a unique undertaking. We traveled to Berlin when they wrapped the Reichstag. They had 1,200 people working on it. And they always complete whatever they start. I don't think anybody else could do it. It's so amazing and I really admire them.

In many ways, what I do is a smaller version of what they do. For example, the *Chandeliers* that we suspended all over the canals of Venice were a similar idea to Christo and Jeanne-Claude's *The Gates* in New York's Central Park since they complement natural surroundings.

We are doing a lot of work in botanical gardens and conservatories all over the world – London, Japan, Finland, Mexico and, of course, the United States. Our work doesn't try to mimic the exotic plants that are exhibited there but, working closely with the people who take care of the greenhouses, we try to complement the natural beauty of the botanical plants and gardens with abstract and organic shapes in the bright colors of which glass is capable.

Steps that I take in my creative process

I work in different ways. Sometimes it's as simple as deciding that day that I want to go to the hot shop and try something new. Or I may set up a special team of glassblowers to work on a specific project. I like working with teams and always have seven or eight people working on a team. Usually, these are guys who work for me full time. If I need special skills I can always call on them. So if I decide that I want to try a new idea, I always have a team that can be working on a particular assignment while I can experiment with something further out.

I started working with a team at a time when nobody else in this country worked with a team. When I went to Europe, I visited some of the glass factories and saw why teamwork was so critical. There were skilled artisans who helped each other. So when I came back to America, I had a much better understanding of how this worked. But it wasn't until several years later that other artists started working with teams. They thought it was not being creative – not the American way to do it. Now almost everybody who works with glass works with a team.

But I like experimenting on my own. It's the exciting part of being creative. It requires making decisions. Once you start making things, you have to decide whether it will lead to something worthwhile. It's always the same decision-making process that all creative people face. As soon as you make one piece, you're already thinking about, "Can this go anywhere? Does this talk to me in some way?" You make another one, and another one, and maybe you're not sure after working on it for a day. You can't really see the glass until the next day anyway, because it needs to go into an oven. So the next morning you come and you look at it and make the final decision.

> ... I like experimenting on my own. It's the exciting part of being creative.

My associates sometimes come to me and say, "I have an idea," which is what I encourage them to do. But many of them are skillful craftsmen rather than being inventive. They give their all to what it is I'm trying to make, and hopefully that experience helps them when they do their own work. I do have quite a few good artists working for me but they tend to keep their own ideas for themselves.

I don't mind that they do. If I were working for someone else, I would probably be thinking of my own work as well.

A lot of the people on my teams do their own work. They go out and rent a facility – not mine, because mine's busy all the time. But there are some hundred glass shops in the Seattle area. In fact, there are now more glassblowers in Seattle than there are in Venice.

My work

Some time ago, I started doing series, like the *Seaforms* and *Baskets*, but I'm doing less and less of that. I didn't start doing commissions until around 1980. Today, most of my work is commissions from museums, conservatories, hotels and residences. We are doing about forty or fifty commissions a year. But I also love doing projects, big projects – like *Chihuly Over Venice*.

Campo della Salute Chandelier, 1996, *Chihuly Over Venice.*
Photo: Russell Johnson

The *Chihuly Over Venice* project was difficult and challenging. It involved hanging fourteen large glass *Chandeliers* over various canals in Venice. It was a great project that required getting permission to hang the *Chandeliers* over the canals. We ultimately did it without permission, and they didn't seem to care.

I just love Venice. But the famous Murano, once the predominant source of fine glassmaking, is probably a quarter of what it was years ago and it is still going down. It's kind of sad. The fact is that there aren't a lot of great glassblowers anymore. The young people don't want to blow glass. They want to go to college and make more money. It used to be, if you were a glassblower, your son became a glassblower. At the turn of the century, you couldn't be a glassblower unless your father was a glassblower. Now that's all changed. Venice is still my favorite city, but I don't go there anymore because of the glass.

One of the most exciting installations I ever did was for the millennium celebration. It was called *Chihuly in the Light of Jerusalem 2000*, and was installed within the Tower of David Museum, which is the Citadel in the old city of Jerusalem. I did the installation as a gift to the people of Jerusalem. It was a large-scale installation and a fantastic project consisting of eighteen or so installations in and around the citadel. It was especially challenging because we had to be understanding of the environment – preserving the stonework and the various ancient structures – we had to be careful about where we were installing.

It was the largest attended exhibition that year. People came from all over Israel to the old city. There was almost always a long line to get into the show. Over a million people came to see that exhibition.

Another project that I always wanted to do – and Jerusalem was a perfect kind of spot for it – was to take blocks of ice from Fairbanks, Alaska, right to the desert. I took something like sixty-four tons of ice and lit the blocks of ice from behind. We had all the electric lights figured out so that people couldn't see the lights, but we could manipulate the colored lights so that they would change the color of the translucent ice any time we wanted, even while the ice was melting.

> I believe that I've made a lasting contribution to the art of glassmaking, if not to art itself.

And as the ice blocks gradually melted – it took about three days – people came to see it as kind of a melting of the tension between Arabs and Jews. There were a lot of Arabs who worked there. So it turned out that a lot of Arabs and a lot of Jews met in the museum. Unfortunately, right after we disassembled the show, things started to go downhill in Israel with the second intifada.

The intifada didn't scare me going over there, but some of my people who had helped unpack and put up the show were concerned about dismantling because of the situation. I didn't want to talk them into it but the Citadel people were confident about taking it down without a problem. I gave the Citadel three of the pieces for cooperating.

Another project that I found very challenging was for the Seattle Opera. They were going to do *Pélleas et Mélisande*, the opera by Claude Debussy. The music is kind of impressionistic and is not considered a very popular opera.

Spike Jenkins, the director of the Seattle Opera, called me and asked if I would like to do the sets for the opera. He said, "Your material and sensibilities are exactly right." I had a hard time turning him down because it seemed like such an interesting project, even though I wasn't familiar with the music at that time. But, I got a CD of the music and some books to read up on it and went to see him to discuss his vision. I finally went ahead and first made all the sets out of glass. There were twelve sets.

Once the sets were designed, we had to decide how we were going to produce them. We couldn't make the final set out of glass because the stage is huge and glass was too heavy and breakable. So we farmed out the different sets to different plastic companies around the country. Most of the pieces were done like inflatables because some of them came down from the ceiling.

I think there were eight performances and I really enjoyed going to all of them to see how people would respond. And a lot of people responded enthusiastically. One of the reasons they wanted to use me for the stage sets was that they were worried about filling the seats for eight *Pelléas et Mélisande* performances and so they advertised that the stage sets were by Chihuly. This worked well and the Seattle Opera House did fill it up.

One of my next projects is at a school in St. Petersburg, Florida, where they are going to rebuild the Arts Center that will include a glass-blowing shop – a nicer one than it already has. It will also include a

Star, Chihuly in the Light of Jerusalem 2000. Photo: Terry Rishel

10,000 sq. ft. Chihuly Collection as a permanent part of the facility. It will probably open in a couple of years.

I consider myself very fortunate to have had an exciting and successful creative career. I believe that I've made a lasting contribution to the art of glassmaking, if not to art itself. And I take pride in my contribution to the art of glassmaking through my involvement with the Pilchuck Glass School.

It is said that when you get your degree in glass, it automatically comes with a one-way ticket to Seattle. This may be slightly exaggerated, but it is a fact that the Pilchuck Glass School has become the starting point of so many careers in the art of glassblowing. And Seattle is sort of artsy. There are a lot of young, hip people in Seattle, and if they are there to attend Pilchuck – they might as well stay there after graduating instead of going anywhere else.

My wish is that I will be around long enough to leave a legacy that will be remembered by generations of glassmakers to come and by people who are inspired by beautiful things.

DANIEL LIBESKIND

Creating reality with architecture

Daniel Libeskind, an international figure in architecture and in design, started as a virtuoso musician. Leaving the field to study architecture, his early career was academic, which changed when he won two high-profile competitions – The Jewish Museum in Berlin and The Imperial War Museum North in Manchester, England. He rose to great fame in 2003 after receiving a commission to create the master plan for the reconstruction of the World Trade Center. He received the 2001 Hiroshima Art Prize – an award given to an artist whose work promotes international understanding and peace, never before given to an architect. His ideas have influenced a generation of architects and those interested in the future development of cities and culture.

I think creativity is something eternal, because it is an encounter with a moment of time.

Creativity is not only the search for the new. It can be a rediscovery of the newness of thousands of years ago, which is still unsurpassed in some way. You can have an encounter with the real world, and in the cross-section of that encounter you have time forward and time backward. So creativity is a kind of philosophical moment.

Of course, creativity is a sense of wonder. Even if you encounter the most banal things that you already have been dealing with, it is a moment of total wonder and you say, "Why this?"

Creativity is being tuned into life

Creativity is constantly alive. It's not God-given that you are alive just because you are breathing. Creativity is that impulse that keeps you in that moment of reality, rather than derailing yourself into dreams or fantasies.

If creativity reaches into the sources of what is real, then architecture, also, has an access to it. Architecture has to reach that source, and out of that discovery, rediscover, reinvent, or invent something that is interesting.

I think to be creative you have to resist taking the easy path. You have to resist the common truths, and you have to take a certain risk. Not risk for the

Daniel Libeskind. *Courtesy of Studio Daniel Libeskind*

sake of risk, but risk to delve into territories that are not well traveled, that are mysterious, so that you do not enter into something that is ready-made and that everybody knows what to do with, but rather make a creative discovery.

> I think to be creative you have to resist taking the easy path.

For me, coming up with ideas is not a linear process. I don't follow a pre-existing path, but sometimes I find myself in the unexpected and often go into realms that are not predicated by any other experience.

When drawing, you can sometimes stumble across a new space. When looking, you can suddenly see something completely evident that was obscure before. Talking to someone, seeing a color, hearing a sound can motivate your action that, in the beginning, doesn't seem to have any rational reason, but in time or in retrospect has logic to it.

What motivates my work?

I think really creative people are not motivated by surface successes. They are motivated by an impulse that is completely real, like the breath of air that you take into your body. Motivation is not something fictitious or something like a "put-on," but true creativity is a desire triggered by something outside you, by reality. And this has almost a divine dimension to it, because the sources are not in you as the creator.

Personally, I've been motivated by many different things: by an angle of light that fell on a wall at a certain time of the day; by names of people who lived at a certain address and are no longer there; by a history that I read in a landscape; by a painting sketched in an attic; by an archeology stripped bare in time; and by an experience that was not apparently easy to get at.

Putting yourself in touch with the spirit of a place – which includes the spirit of people, not just of ghosts, but the spirit of life that is there across time – that

> Realizing a project is like orchestration and choreography, with a huge array of different players and dancers, directors and producers.

is the source of architecture for me.

I think music and architecture are very closely related. Even though I'm not a musician anymore, not a virtuoso performer as I used to be, I still feel that I'm doing something not much different from music. By drawing and creating a building, I utilize similar muscles, similar parts of my brain and similar ways of moving my hands. Realizing a project is like orchestration and choreography, with a huge array of different players and dancers, directors and producers. The logic of building a building or master planning an area of a city is much like the role of a conductor – all the players are independent but must play or dance in harmony.

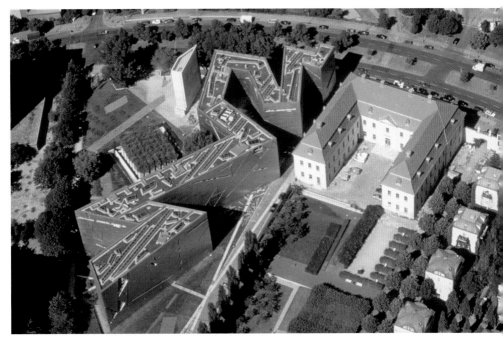

Jewish Museum Berlin, aerial view. *Courtesy of Studio Daniel Libeskind*

I don't just sit at a desk and start drawing a building. It has to come to me. You have to be engaged with something that is more powerful than you are, and kind of struggle with it. It's something very strange, and the give and take in the process is the kind of creative process that's not easily explained.

My early years

My parents were Holocaust survivors, first under the occupation of the Nazis and then in Russian concentration camps, and yet they had a view of life that went far beyond the terrible atrocities they suffered. They taught me by not only talking to me, but by the spirit of their personalities.

When my mother was in the Gulag in Siberia and was abused by the commandant in his office, she picked up an inkwell and threw it at him and at the portrait of Stalin, which hung behind him. He could have killed her right then and there, but he didn't. His shock was too great. So it's the spirit and strength of a personality that is valuable, and certainly without my parents, and without their traditions, I would never have been who I am.

My parents always encouraged me. They were very open-minded – they didn't expect me to be X, Y or Z. They believed in me. Even if others would see something as a failure, my mother would say, "Don't listen to them. Do what you believe in." And if you're lucky to depend on someone who believes in you, then you also have a much easier time to do things.

I grew up as a child in the grayness of postwar Communist Poland and then, via the vibrant colors of Israel, I came to New York at the age of thirteen. Like all typical immigrants, I didn't know the English language.

I fell in love with the creativity of New York. Growing up in New York gives you a creative injection, a tremendous boost to your creativity, because everywhere you look, and every moment of your life, you're challenged in a way that is not imaginable almost anywhere else.

I used to spend hours at museums, at concerts, at free lectures, in parks, at all the beautiful places that are available and accessible.

My musical education was an important influence. When you're a performer on a stage, music does not tolerate mistakes or wrong notes. Later on, I studied at Bronx High School of Science because I loved the sciences and mathematics. The ability to bring together the arts, mathematics and the scientific disciplines with architecture was something that I've continued to develop.

When I studied architecture at The Cooper Union I had wonderful teachers, some of whom in many ways were somewhat dogmatic. They had very strong ideas and were very ideological and in a strange way I could rebel against them. I'm lucky to have had such a great education. I consider education the most important thing for creativity, because if you have a mediocre education, with teachers who don't really care, who don't have any ideas of their own, who are just working nine to five, you are not encouraged to explore your own realms of creativity.

I went through a rigorous and punishing educational system in Poland under Communism and I studied the Talmud in Israel, yet I still believe that creativity has to do with freedom. To some extent, even though we might think of ourselves as free, we are not really free, but the most important thing is to try to get free, which is the essence of creativity.

My life on the move

To be spontaneous is part of the creative process, along with doing things that to others may seem totally irrational or even stupid. My family and I have moved fourteen or fifteen times across the world, eight times across the Atlantic. Some people wondered whether we were with the military or with the diplomatic corps. Of course we were not and never had anyone paying for these multiple moves. A bit insane!!

I had a lifetime tenured position as the head of the Cranbrook Academy of Art architecture school. But on a moment's inspiration, I decided that I should leave this tenured, safe, academic position to do something totally different.

Interior window, Jewish Museum Berlin. *Photo: Herb Meyers*

When we moved to Italy, we had no family in Italy and we were not Italians. There was no rational reason for moving there, since I had a good job at Cranbrook and had to support a family. But something compelled me to move there – perhaps the depth of Italian culture that I had read about and had experienced to some degree. People thought we were completely insane and, in a way, we probably were at that time. But I think instinctively that you have to follow a certain path.

When, later, we moved from Italy to Berlin, again on the spur of the moment, people again thought we were mad. We had won the Berlin Jewish Museum competition, but there was only money for the first prize and you don't normally move somewhere just because you win a competition. But, as difficult as it was for us to move again, I wanted to become part of Germany.

Being the victor of a competition in architecture doesn't mean very much, usually only a few headlines in the press. To actually build a building, you really need support – not just economically, but politically and socially – and there was very little support in Berlin especially after the Wall fell in 1989. The Jewish Museum in Berlin had no client, no money and no political program for many years.

My belief in creating reality

I had never practiced architecture before and the Jewish Museum was my first project. My wife Nina calls me a late bloomer and even though I trained as an architect, I was, up to that time, an educator. So this was the first building that I ever constructed.

But I learned that with a building – not just the Jewish Museum in Berlin, but any building – if you have an idea, the idea becomes the reality. The idea becomes the creative force helping to propel the project into a realistic realm.

But I believed that the actions of an architect – a drawing, a collage, a model – are a way to create reality. It is not just a response to reality, but it is almost like a flame that somehow burns a path through a dusty field.

I moved to Berlin before the Wall came down. I did a drawing of the Jewish Museum as a kind of starburst – the Star of David – and I remember that I crossed out the Berlin Wall. I did so because I wanted to make the point that in matters of Jewish history there was no wall dividing East from West. It was late 1988 and I believed at that moment that the Wall disappeared, because I drew over it, and it meant nothing anymore. How amazing it was that the Wall did come down! Without being delusional, I want to believe that crossing that wall out in my drawing, with all that positive energy, helped to bring the Wall down.

> ...the actions of an architect – a drawing, a collage, a model – are a way to create reality. It is not just a response to reality, but it is almost like a flame that somehow burns a path through a dusty field.

Actually, after the German reunification in 1991, the Berlin Senate threatened to scrap the Jewish Museum project entirely. Had they done so, it would have been almost impossible to make the project a reality. But faith is closely related to both wonder and creativity. Believing in something is an important part of it and, eventually, the project was realized.

The Jewish Museum took a very long time and I could never have done it without the creativity of my wife and partner. She is not an architect, but she is creative by understanding things that I could not understand – what politicians were saying and what the public was saying.

How I create

Architecture is more a storytelling profession than anything else. You have to connect things like music, literature, architecture and poetry, and see architecture as a storytelling sequence. Just like any story, you have to find a source, listen to someone and transmit that story, and you have to inscribe yourself into the story.

There is no real hierarchy in the office. Although it's a big office, it's not run like a corporation. Our office is made up of many creative teams, each team with four or five people. Each part of the creative team works freely, but I am involved with each project, hands on. It's not as if I do a sketch and I hand it over as if there were some sort of machine that processes the sketch. It's having the love for a project from the beginning to the end. Nothing is unimportant. Everything is concentric. As far as I'm concerned, there are no major and minor things in architecture, because the quality of the floor, the ceiling, or even the door handles is as important as the big idea of what it looks like on the street.

> You have to connect things like music, literature, architecture and poetry...

For an architectural project, you have to absorb what the needs are and you have to learn everything you can about what the client thinks and what the place is about. Then you have to put yourself on a wavelength with other issues that the client hasn't told you about – needs that are not apparent.

And how do you do that? You do that by going there, by being there, by connecting yourself with the place. Sometimes you connect yourself to the place with a very obscure method like digging in a place where there seems to be no water, or no life – but you instinctively believe you will find something that you are pursuing – something meaningful. I have often gone off on an oblique tangent to a project in order to go back into the center of it.

To me, every project has a set of signs, and they are everywhere. You have to be able to create a text out of these signs – windows, colors, shadows, light, people's faces, secrets told to you, the geometries of space. You become almost a soothsayer, a diviner, because you have to follow things that are not on anyone else's map.

I achieve this while working with a lot of very creative people. It's very important to give them credit, because without their creativity, I couldn't do what I'm doing. My associates take the ideas and they challenge my notions: Can this be done? Should this not be done? How can it be done better? So I'm very fortunate to work with these creative colleagues, friends from all over the world.

The emotions of architecture

It is often that I meet people by accident, or by chance, who give me a new way of seeing the world. They could be people I talk to on the subway or people I encounter elsewhere who give me a new way of looking at things.

Even people who are not alive today can inspire me creatively. I find them "alive," and I have "conversations" with them. For example, I love Michelangelo and Bromine and I love the colors of Vermeer. I love the structural logic of Picasso, and of Mies van der Rohe. I become engaged because I think those works are still alive and I'm challenged by them all the time.

Then there are times when ideas are triggered by a poem or by a piece of music. But it's more like looking at the nebulae up in the sky and seeing some cluster that has a certain shape that brings together all sorts of contributory experiences. And then, something falls out of the hand, eye or mind – an idea that is very bold and is searching for reality.

I have always found that if I force myself to do something, or if I'm required to create something on somebody's schedule, I'm not going to be creative. But if I'm truly caught up by a project, then I am creative, and it becomes real. If you don't love doing it, then it's just a job, and you might as well not do it, because it will never turn out to be anything that you would be proud of.

I have been involved in many wonderful projects. Ground Zero – the area in New York where the Twin Towers once stood – is a project that I continue to work on despite its huge complexities and difficulties. Again, I think that emotion is part of creativity and there's got to be passion despite all the odds. You have to be a believer. And I'm a believer in navigating through the Ground Zero labyrinth of conflicting stakeholders and staying involved until you end up with something good. You have got to stay the course and believe that something better will emerge. That's a project that I truly believe in.

The creative viewpoint for Ground Zero was very palpable. I had been working on the project, absorbing all the complex technical information, which is an endless stream of knowledge that you need to have to create this space. I went down into the pit on a cold, rainy day in October 2002. Of all the architects at the briefing, I was the only one who said I'd like to go down there when the Port Authority offered to do so.

My world changed as I physically experienced the slurry wall, its power and resilience in the light of New York. I imagined myself again arriving on the ship with my mother and my sister and seeing the Statue of Liberty. And the whole project came to me in a glimpse, in a second.

I asked somebody to give me a telephone, and I called my studio and I said, "Drop everything that we've been doing. I have a totally other idea." A complete project had emerged. It was that instant encounter with that physical wall, with the sky, close to the bedrock, close to the space where thousands had died, and I saw the world in a different way.

The design for Ground Zero has gone through a myriad of changes, because architecture and creativity are evolutionary in their nature. But the logic and symbolism of the master plan have stayed intact and the integrity of the plan will be delivered to the public. I know that there are many who are skeptical and do not believe in it, but I believe in it, and I think good things will happen from it.

A project that has just opened in Denver is an embodiment of the energy of the American West. It's a building that in some way was inspired by the Rocky Mountains. I looked down at those peaks and valleys from the plane as we were flying over them and I saw those incredible formations that were more eloquent than any architecture I've ever seen. I thought that the building in Denver should really express the tectonic energy that gave rise to where this city grew. And I created a building that I think mirrors the character and the intensity of that landscape, which is not only physical, but also mental.

I was not only lucky to do that building, but also was able to create a large public plaza, condominiums, and the kind of life that connected the museum to the city in a new way with a whole new urban space.

That's the wonder of creativity. Initially, the competition program asked for only the museum. But it was a public building and also the garage for a thousand cars. I thought, "This is not good enough. Why don't I dream up something fantastic? People could live there and the garage could be screened by housing, towers, retail, and a new plaza for the city."

Lo and behold, the museum authorities and the public authorities of Denver embraced the idea. All this happened as the result of a series of sketches and models when, initially, there seemed to be no such need and nobody had even thought of it.

Why I believe in consensus

I think creativity is not just your own creativity. If you are able to tap into the

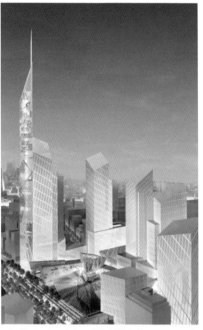

Architectural rendering of World Trade Center master site plan, presented by the Lower Manhattan Development Corporation and the Port Authority of New York and New Jersey in 2003. *Courtesy of Studio Daniel Libeskind*

creative world of every person and unlock that creativity, then, like a sponge, you will be able to absorb it and create something that is really good.

I believe in democracy. Creativity cannot flourish in a totalitarian environment where somebody is dictating to somebody else what to do, and what not to do. Many dictators have produced beautiful objects, but I'm not at all interested in these, because I don't see creativity as apart from the human soul. If the soul is not implicated, then it's only surface forms, and that's not impressive to me. I believe in the public process, and I believe in consensus, and I don't believe it weakens architecture.

Many people criticize me for this belief in consensus, but I actually enjoy it when a project is transformed and it has life. The Jewish Museum in Berlin went through a whole series of transformations, due to cost and to many different issues. But I think that is what gives a project a life. I would hate a project where the drawings were exactly the same in the beginning as at the end. To me, that would be a very abstract and not very good project. But you still have to stick with your convictions and vision. If the project is rich enough in ideas and creativity, then the soul will remain.

Left: Denver Art Museum forms the centerpiece of the new cultural district for the city. *Courtesy of Studio Daniel Libeskind. Photo: Bitter Bredt*

I have had some tough clients, who are only interested in making money and you have to fight for what you believe in architecturally. I understand they want to maximize profits and I don't think that this is always bad. It's part of the challenge.

Look, if you didn't have a frame, you couldn't make a painting. An architect works within a frame that is public, economic and social. Many architects think, "Get rid of the frame – have someone who gives you a lot of money and you do what you want." I actually think a frame is good. That's what makes architecture so much fun and so challenging.

I love the challenge, perhaps because I came from a very working-class background. My parents never lived an opulent life. I think that not having luxuries becomes a value of life that is honorable. I think that if I were offered the choice of a piece of gold or a piece of wood, I would take the piece of wood.

My obscure path to creativity

I often meet people who in their profession have to do things that they don't particularly enjoy, and then they try to do something else. I'm really lucky because everything I do is interesting to me.

I have a loving family and wife and children, yet I feel that I also need time to be away from everything and do nothing. That time is really very important for me. It's not a time of escapism, but a time that I use to create buildings – which I do when delving into a poem, doing some music, walking on a street or just lying under a tree.

I have never had a defined goal and I followed a pretty obscure path. I always wanted to do architecture and drew and read and lots of other things. Some people thought it was a waste of time but I believe you have to forge a path that has no specific goal and stick to the path. You don't really know where you are going, but as long as you are not derailed from your path by being pushed to the left or right, and maintain your balance on this path, you'll be drawn to something. You don't know exactly what it is that you're drawn to, but it's like a magnet on the other side and you simply follow it.

The path is a search for the creative moment where you do not fall into a formula, nor stick too closely to what you've learned from experience, nor be deluded by your successes, nor pay attention to what other people are saying about your work.

People write to me a lot to tell me that my buildings are connected with very profound experiences for them because my buildings are very personal. And I think that's precisely what architecture means to me – not a lot of concrete and glass and big steel columns – but a kind of communication. You're telling a story to someone, and there has to be the human response to it – a mutual resonance.

I'm thrilled when people tell me that they've had profoundly moving emotions at some of my museums or that they have new ideas, and that new things have happened to them as a result of visiting and being inside one of my buildings.

If creativity were to disappear, people would only be satisfied with what already exists. There would not be that creative spark of working on something that's not yet available. Because, in a way, that's what creativity is. It's a reality that does not really exist. But just because it doesn't exist, doesn't mean it's not real. It's there. It just has not been introduced as an object in the world or as something that you can put your hands on.

Creativity, to me, is the future of the world. Creativity means individuality. If we lose creativity, we also lose individuality. And if individuality is lost, then the world is finished – it becomes just a machine. The human spirit has to prevail.

NANDAN NILEKANI

Visualizing the future of global business

Nandan Nilekani is the chief executive officer and president of Infosys, with headquarters in Bangalore, India and over 66,000 employees worldwide. Along with changing the domestic software industry of India, he has led the company to pioneer the concept of outsourcing for corporations all over the world. He was one of the youngest entrepreneurs to join twenty global leaders on the prestigious World Economical Forum Foundation Board, and is regarded by Time *magazine as one of the 100 most influential people in the world. His creative thinking on global initiatives has made him a world spokesman on how business will function in the future.*

I think there are different kinds of creativity. Classically, we have thought of creativity in the artistic sense, in terms of art, music, and literature. But I think there is a lot of creativity in business today, and sometimes we can underestimate and undervalue this kind of creativity.

To my mind, a lot of business creativity has to do with visualizing a future that others don't see. In business, success comes when you see something – you see a pattern, and maybe you look at different things that are not really related – and when you look across those things, you suddenly see a kernel of an idea. And that has the potential of making an impact. Then you figure out how to get there.

I think that business creativity is in understanding different trends and different incidents that are completely unconnected in some ways and saying, "Hey, maybe if we take these two or three things together, this is the likely way things will go. If we do the right thing, we can take advantage of that."

Therefore, good creativity in business requires lateral thinking. It requires you to be able see a pattern of potential opportunity across many disparate things.

How my company got started

A good example of creative thinking is our business history. We started Infosys in 1981 and were a very small company for the first ten years of our existence. But in 1991, several things happened and not many people saw the pattern of those things happening.

Nandan M. Nilekani. *Courtesy of Infosys Technologies Inc.*

First and suddenly, the Indian business environment became free to do business – what we call the "liberalization" of the Indian economy. That's one thing that happened.

The second thing that happened was that new technology made it possible to use things like earth stations and satellites that could sit in India to do work for clients in the United States. This was an exciting new development. You couldn't do this before, but technology made it possible.

> ... new technology made it possible to use things like earth stations and satellites that could sit in India to do work for clients in the United States.

The third thing that happened was that western customers began to see the value in using Indian resources and Indian skills to do some of their work. People like Jack Welch, the CEO of General Electric at the time, and others actually visited India back in the 1980s to explore this.

The fourth thing that happened was that the Indian capital markets became free and it was much easier for companies like ours to raise money in those markets.

When you added all these things together, I think the key insight was that people are going to want more and more of this. More companies will want to work in India with Indian talent, and so forth, and they will look for partners to work with. And they will come to India to look for these partners.

And what is it that they will look for? They will look for companies that have stature and a presence. They will look for companies that have a campus where people are able to work, and that have investment in technology. So we said, "OK, let's build a campus." You might think this is a trivial idea, but in 1991 it was a big idea.

So Infosys went public, raised money and built a very nice campus, like a university. We didn't want it to look like a corporate office or a tall building. We said, "Let's make it low slung, one or two stories high and, just like a university campus, sprawled out with a lot of greenery and all that. And make sure that it's well equipped with technology."

That was a creative idea and that actually gave the momentum, because we built it ahead of the curve. We didn't build it with orders already in our hands. We said, "We know that the business is going to happen and the trade is going to happen. If we are there at the right time in the right place, with a great campus, that will help to drive the business to us."

And that is a classic example of creativity – thinking about a future development that nobody had laid out before. If you can visualize a potential of something that is huge when it's not there yet, and you have the desire to bridge that gap, you can make the potential the reality.

How we changed the way people work

Historically, in the service business, people have worked in an informal way. I mean, if you had this office with 500 people doing ten different things, and they all sort of figured out among themselves what to do, then you really wouldn't know who did what.

We changed this way of working. We said, "Look, we should really take advantage of where the best talent is, where the best skills are, where the best education is, where the best knowledge is, and so forth." To do that, you need to figure out how to make this work on a global basis. You need to figure out a way to demarcate and desegregate the work so that everybody knows who is doing what. And you have to figure out how to do the transactions with people over a distance.

But setting it up this way changes the whole paradigm of working. The advantage is that you have a much more powerful way of structuring your business, so that it's different in each location. That gives you a new degree of freedom, which is actually the source of our particular advantage.

I don't think that when we founded the company, we had any idea that by now, we would have over 60,000 employees, $2 billion in revenue, and that we would become a global brand.

It would really change the notion of how the world works. And that's a big idea.

Many years ago we tried to get into the hardware industry – manufacturing telecommunications products. That was a complete failure. What this taught us was that we were really good at software and we were really good at intellectual capital kind of work, but we did not know how to make things and sell them. So now we stick to our knitting.

> It would really change the notion of how the world works. And that's a big idea.

My earlier years

I was born in Bangalore, India, which is where I live today, and where I spent my early education up to the age of 12. Bangalore is where we have our corporate headquarters. Then I moved to a smaller town and lived there for five or six years, and did the rest of my schooling.

At the age of 18, I went to an engineering college called the Indian Institute of Technology – IIT – one of the very famous colleges in India. It's like MIT in the United States. I spent five years there, which really were the turning point in my life. The good thing about IIT is that the best and the brightest go there, since getting into IIT is an arduous process with a huge exam, and not many people get through it.

So, that way, you automatically enter into an environment with many other bright and talented people. For one thing, it's very competitive and, two, it creates its own energy because there are so many bright young people. It's a residential place, where you all stay together and you develop strong relationships. It's also a place where you get to participate in a wide variety of activities outside the classroom – like sports and theater – and you get a very all-round kind of exposure. That was very critical for me in my developing years, so that when I came out of that college, I was much better equipped to deal with starting a business.

> It's more about building a culture where people are intrigued with an idea and are free to run with it.

Why new ideas are important

Assuming that I'm a creative person – or if that's what some people think I am – I can't attribute this to any particular sort of genesis or any particular source. But the juxtaposition of different things in new ways to create new value has always intrigued me. When you juxtapose different things, you can suddenly create enormous opportunities that people have not thought of before. And that is what I find very intriguing, that is what motivates me, although I can't say where the root of that comes from.

Employees of Infosys form groups to develop new ideas.
Courtesy of Infosys Technologies Inc.

Motivation comes not so much from the money, but from living in a world where there are so many things happening, and if you can put them all together, you can create enormous value, whether business value, or social value, or transformational value. Looking at these various opportunities and putting them together can create some value that makes a difference.

When we started our business in 1981, three or four strong beliefs influenced us. One was that we believed that software – the broad area of software development, intellectual capital – was going to be a growth area. We said the world needs more software. And that was fairly evident, even in those days.

The second thing we said was that we live in a part of the world where there is enormous talent, but the talent is not yet really leveraged. Its potential is not being used. There is a way we can use this talent differently.

The third thing we said was that we need a really high-quality, professional company in this area, because that will help attract talent. It was all about having the best brains.

And the fourth thing we said was that ultimately we'll be able to use technology to do it anywhere. These were the driving ideas.

Some of the ideas came from our customers. Customers are a huge source of ideas, because customers are constantly pushing us to do more things for them, more innovative things and more value creation. So I think listening to customers is of huge importance.

And a lot of ideas come from within, from our own people. Because when you have so many bright people who are working with technology, working with clients and traveling the world, they will see something that is innovative that we can use. So customers and employees are the two big sources of ideas for us.

You can't predict where the idea will come from, nor can you centralize ideas. But you can create an ecosystem where ideas flourish. It's more about building a culture where people are intrigued with an idea and are free to run with it.

We feel that you can't be too bureaucratic and rigid to evaluate an idea. If somebody, or if a business unit, has an idea for a new service, they just find some money and do it on their own. But if the idea needs a lot more corporate sponsorship, they will then put it up to a bunch of people who will decide whether it's a good idea and, if it is, allocate money for it. Then they can move from their everyday tasks to pursue it.

The future of work

We now have an idea on a transformational message that we can communicate to our clients. And we think it's a big idea, so there is a dedicated group looking at how to turn that into reality.

The idea that is really keeping us occupied, and which I'm enjoying tremendously, is trying to demonstrate how companies will look in the future – *the future of work*. And this goes back to what I think we have done, which is to create a new way of working.

Now, if you extrapolate that, and if you look at what is happening in the world in terms of technology, globalization, competition and so forth, it means that firms will have to redesign themselves to function in this new, so-called, "flat world." And because we are an example

... firms will have to redesign themselves to function in this new, so-called, "flat world."

of such a firm, we believe that we are the best people to actually help other companies become like us in the way they structure themselves. We believe that is a very strong concept that we can take to market, and it's something that positions us as a transformational company.

We find that when we put this idea to customers, they really like it. They want us to come back with more ideas. There's a lot of work ahead to take this concept and convert it into real substance that customers can benefit from. But it's a very exciting idea, and right now I'm occupied with what we need to do to convert this idea into reality.

It's not global in the classical sense and it's not just about selling abroad or manufacturing abroad. It's really about restructuring the inside of the firm to take advantage of the best information and best people, independent of location and independent of distance.

We identify two or three business units and say, "In your industry, what does this concept mean? What does this mean for a bank? What does this mean for a communication company?" And we are actually drilling down to come back to them, saying, "Well, this is what it means in terms of what you sell, whom you sell to, how you sell it, and what value you create." And so we will help them develop the road map to get there. There's a lot of new thinking in that.

We created new paradigm

We think our contribution is far more than just being a company. In the past, businesses in India were either government companies or multinational companies – the IBMs of the world – or they were family-owned companies. The notion that a bunch of disparate people could come together and create a company was either unknown or not thought to be very plausible. So we created a whole new paradigm.

Now there are better jobs and wealth and all that sort of thing. But also, by being creative in the business sense, we are the first generation entrepreneurial company in India in the real successful sense. Although there are others, nobody has reached our size and scale.

We call that the democratization of entrepreneurship.

Anybody can now say, "I could be like these guys. I can start a company and do something." Our example opened the opportunity for many people to think that they can be entrepreneurs, and that's a big change in the mindset.

We demonstrated that you can run a company with very high ethical standards – honesty, transparency, accountability and all that – and make money. This again was a very strong message that convinced many other people to follow our model of planning companies with high corporate governing standards. That also has huge impact.

There is another aspect that I believe is very important. I'm absolutely convinced that India is the most democratic country in our region. A lot of people believed that democracy and economic development were incompatible, at least in Asia. And for many years economic growth was very slow. People blamed this on democracy, saying, "Look, when you have a democracy, you can't grow. You can't have the luxury of discussion and you need authoritarian leadership that will get things done quickly. Bring in a dictator or something and you will grow faster. Once you raise people's standard of living, you can then grant democracy to them."

Fortunately, India, a country with many different religions and much diversity, didn't choose to go that way, but instead chose to be a democracy with complete voting rights for everybody.

India has had 8 percent growth for the last three years. This is proving a very important point, that democracy and economic growth are not incompatible. In fact, they can go hand in hand. Democracy is not only able to deal with diversity of religion, caste, and all such issues, but it also acts as a pressure wall to remove the frustrations of inequity. Because having the right to vote, you can choose the best people and throw out the worst. I think it's now becoming clear that it is really the right model in the long term for encouraging and creating new ideas. And that is a big win.

Left: The rotunda that houses Infosys' central library in Bangalore, India. The rotunda is currently the largest in Asia. *Courtesy of Infosys Technologies Inc.*

ERICA JONG

Seducing her own demons

Erica Jong, the author and educator, is best known for her first novel, Fear of Flying, *which was published in 1973 shortly after she graduated Barnard College and Columbia University's Graduate Facilities, where she had studied eighteenth-century English literature. The novel created a sensation with its frank treatment of a woman's sexual desires. She is the author of eight novels and several have been worldwide best-sellers. She has taught literature and writing at various universities and her works have appeared all over the world, being as popular in Eastern Europe, Japan, China and Asia as they have been in the United States and Western Europe. In 1998 she was honored with the United Nations Award for Excellence in Literature.*

Creativity is very mysterious. I think that a creative person is someone who sees the world differently, and does not accept the structures that most people unthinkingly accept.

Most people are given certain routines in school, certain routines in growing up, and they assume that that's the way the world is. Other people are absolutely born questioning everything. Or they have the need not only to question everything, but also to write, or compose, or paint their version of the world. The way they see the world is so specific and so different from what they are told by authority figures, they have no choice but to make it their own. But I cannot tell you where that comes from.

> Real creativity consists of seeing the world differently from the way other people see it, and being compelled to share that with others.

People have been looking for what constitutes creativity for thousands and thousands of years, and I think that the word "creativity" is horribly overused. If you go to Los Angeles, you will discover that there are creative accountants, creative dress designers, creative everything. It's become a kind of cliché. I think it's the most overused word in the dictionary, and most of the people who apply it to themselves are not creative at all.

Real creativity consists of seeing the world differently from the way other people see it, and being compelled to share that with others.

Erica Jong. *Photo: James J. Kriegsmann*

Composers hear music that other people do not hear. Artists see designs and shapes and things that nobody else sees.

Creative people tend to cluster in families. I don't know what the average parent is like. I only know what my parents were like. My mother was an artist. My father was a musician. So I grew up in a house where people painted and wrote and played music, and it always seemed to me to be a very normal thing to do.

Most of the members of my family sketched and painted. Even the people in my family who were not professional writers always wrote. They wrote wonderful letters, they wrote doggerel on birthdays, they wrote song lyrics for the hell of it. It was not considered odd. And everybody read books.

My grandfather was an artist, and he was incapable of taking a walk without sketching. If he walked through Central Park, he would stop at the zoo and sketch the animals. If he sat on a subway train, he would sketch the people sitting opposite him. Why was he motivated to do that? I really don't know, but he had a very clear picture of the world, and it was a compulsion for him to get it down on paper.

So I suppose growing up in a family like that predisposes you to consider those normal activities.

Anthony Burgess, the writer, was also a composer of music, and he could not get through a day without composing a certain number of bars of music and a certain number of words. Whether it was music, or essays, film scripts, oratorios, novels – he needed to write every day of his life.

What motivates such creative activity is very mysterious even to the people who do it.

My thoughts about my writing

I guess what motivates me is sheer grit. When you are in the flow state where the words are coming and time is suspended – which comes relatively rarely, perhaps one day out of a hundred – it's the most blissful feeling on earth. On the other days, it is just sheer torture and you feel like Sisyphus climbing up a mountain. But you stay with it because of those rare moments when it feels completely heavenly and out of time. You also stay with it because it's what you do. You've made up your mind that this is the contribution you have to make to the world. You feel that this is what you do best and you feel most yourself when you're doing it.

It's never been my lot to get total approval from everybody. People who write in accepted forms – forms that were handed down by others – may get a lot more approval than people who are inventing new forms. I've gotten applause and rotten tomatoes in pretty much equal measure. I've always had my fair share of brickbats. And I understand that that's one of the prices you pay for being a pioneer.

It never changes. With my latest book, I've had dozens of the most ecstatic reviews of my life and also some of the nastiest. The ecstatic ones outweigh the nasty ones, but the nasty ones are really apoplectic. The persons writing them seem to be personally offended by my existence on the planet.

People get enraged at me because they think women should not write about the things I write about, because the things that I write about, in some way, break with their notion of what a woman should be.

> People get enraged at me because they think women should not write about the things I write about, because the things that I write about, in some way, break with their notion of what a woman should be.

The people who criticize me don't seem to be criticizing my writing, but rather reserve a special enmity for me as a human being, as if I'm bringing American civilization or world civilization to its knees. Perhaps that has to do with being a woman. Perhaps it has to do with being outspoken or being known for sexuality. I'm not really sure what it has to do with, but nobody is indifferent to my work.

So I'm used to controversy. I have no choice. My work has always elicited a great deal of controversy, and I no longer feel demolished by it, or silenced by it as I did when I was younger. People who get apoplectic when they hear my name seem to have problems in other areas. They seem to be fearful of pleasure and are unable to enjoy themselves. We live in a very puritanical culture where somebody who tangibly enjoys life is looked upon as a threat.

The reaction is very different in other parts of the world. There, people are usually much more appreciative. Although I have to say that *Seducing the Demon*, which has been a national best-seller, has gotten a very warm response and rave reviews in a lot of places. The few places that have bitterly attacked me seem to be attacking not the book, but my very being.

Looking for ideas

Seducing the Demon is a memoir about writing. Actually, a lot of things about creativity are better said in that book than I could ever say otherwise. I was working for about fifteen years on a book for fledgling writers that was essentially a book of meditations. Writers work all by themselves, and in the morning when you sit down to work at the computer or a yellow legal pad, it's very, very lonely, and you need something to get yourself started.

An actor who goes into a reading has a director and other colleagues there. A journalist generally has somebody to interview or something to witness and report about. A musician is often working with other musicians. But a writer is alone, alone, alone, and it is a very, very lonely profession.

So *Seducing the Demon* began as a book of meditations to get creative people started every day – to sort of jolt them out of not writing into writing. As I was writing it, it changed into something very different. It turned into a piece of my autobiography as a writer.

I think that's true of all my books. The most interesting thing about writing books is that each book becomes a complete self-exploration, self-analysis, and when you come to the end of it, you are aware of things that you never were aware of before. That's why, no matter how arduous the process is, it's always rewarding.

In *Seducing the Demon*, I write about the ineffability of the process of writing and how, in retrospect, the process is known only to you. If somebody were to tell you, "Oh, I had this creative idea, and then I decided to put it down on paper, or canvas, or notes or whatever, and it turned out exactly as I anticipated," you would know that person had no talent.

The person who really has ability and talent will never say that, because the process of creating the work is a process of discovery, both inner and outer discovery. It cannot be forced and you don't know where it comes from, but in surrendering yourself to the process – you make discoveries.

At the end of the process – which you're always very reluctant to end – you may look back and say, "Oh, that's where I was going." But before that, you never really know.

> ... the process of creating the work is a process of discovery, both inner and outer discovery. It cannot be forced and you don't know where it comes from, but in surrendering yourself to the process – you make discoveries.

I actually don't go *looking* for ideas – ideas well up in me. I often work on them for years and years and years without finding the right form. Many of my novels have begun with a few lines in a notebook, which I didn't know how to develop. And then, five years later I'm flipping through the notebook and suddenly it occurs to me that I know how to develop it. The whole process of what you would call creativity happens underground. That's what is so exciting about it – you never really know where it comes from.

You may put down a few lines, saying, "Oh, this doesn't work," put it aside, and then come up with it some time later when it's grown wings and claws and secrets. Suddenly you say, "Oh, wow, maybe I should play with this."

My third novel, *Fanny*, was set in eighteenth-century England. It started with a line "I, Fanny Hackabout Jones, having been blessed with long life, do make

Original 1973 cover. Over 6.5 million copies of *Fear of Flying* were sold in the US alone. Around the world there are 12.5 million copies in print in twenty-seven languages. *Photo: Richard Gerstman*

this testament for my only daughter, Belinda." It was written in the sound of an eighteenth-century woman who might have been a contemporary of Henry Fielding, the author of *Tom Jones*, or a contemporary of Jonathan Swift. When I first wrote it, I thought, "Oh, this doesn't work. This is ridiculous." And so I put it in a drawer. Six months later I came upon it again and I thought, "What an interesting idea. Let me play with this and see if I can sustain it."

I wrote about fifty pages, and got really excited about it. Then I sat rereading eighteenth-century novels, and hearing the cadence of the language, and really got into the idea of writing a mock eighteenth-century novel, a kind of female *Tom Jones*.

Fanny took about five years to write. It involved a great deal of research. I wrote it in an eighteenth-century language of my own invention. I checked every word against the Oxford English Dictionary to make sure it was a word in use in 1728, or the mid-eighteenth century. I don't think I'd ever do that again, because it doesn't really matter. Usages of words have changed considerably since the mid-eighteenth century. But I was such a stickler, that I wanted all the words to be words that Fanny herself might have spoken if she was really born in the reign of Queen Anne and if she really had lived in the age of revolution, which is what I imagined in the book.

Eighteenth-century language was my specialty in graduate school. I was always in love with the satirists of the eighteenth century. And it was a period that I felt extremely comfortable in, and I knew a lot about it from a scholarly point of view. I was also on my way to getting a Ph.D. during the period. So it was a period of time that was important to me.

But to go from that to actually inventing a heroine of that age is a whole other story. It was a very complex novel of nearly a thousand pages with thousands of characters whose stories you have to keep in your head.

It wasn't really possible to work on other books or write poetry during that five-year period. But when you're engrossed in a novel and the novel has a lot of characters, and you're writing it in an invented language, it's not easy to work on anything else. I could not even write journalism, or essays, or reviews at that time because I was so engrossed in that particular book.

I'm not a strict outliner, but every few days I'll put down notes for where the plot is going and where the different characters are going. I never really have the arc of the plot until I have written two or three hundred pages, and then I start to see what the arc is. And I rewrite demonically. The great thing about writing is that you can rewrite endlessly. In fact, you can rewrite so endlessly you never give up a manuscript. That's a danger, too. You may not know when something is finished until they sort of grab it out of your hands.

Creativity vs. criticism

I think probably the most important thing I do is my poetry. I always write poetry when poetry comes to me. When I was a young person and published two volumes of poetry, I won all the major poetry prizes – prizes that were also won by Sylvia Plath and W.S. Merwin. Despite that, and despite the fact that I have continued writing poetry, the poets have disowned me, because I became a successful novelist. Poets are not generous and they tend to be very jealous. They don't love you for sticking with poetry, but they hate you for being able to sell novels.

> ... despite the fact that I have continued writing poetry, the poets have disowned me

In my general view, the most difficult thing about functioning in the world of "creativity" – and I use that word in quotes – is that some creative people are so mean and niggardly. And they wish the worst for you. There is a great deal of *Schadenfreude*. That probably is the most difficult thing about being a functioning artist.

If you think of Tennessee Williams, one of our greatest playwrights – he couldn't open a play during the last few years of his life without people saying what a train wreck he was. The same with Arthur Miller, who I knew for many years, and whose work was being done all over the world – in China, in Yugoslavia, in Russia – where he was appreciated and loved. But every time he opened a play in New York, people would jump all over him to try to close the play as soon as possible. As soon as Arthur died, they suddenly confessed that he was a great playwright. Tennessee Williams' situation was similar.

Which work is better than the other is not for contemporaries to decide, because contemporaries are too close to it to really know what will last. I doubt that Mozart's contemporaries had any idea what a great opera *The Magic Flute* was. It opened in a very down-and-out kind of vaudeville place. People were mystified by the Masonic imagery, as often we have been mystified by it. Certainly, nobody thought of it as his greatest opera.

> It's that excitement, that kind of shivering feeling, that something moves you. That weirdly spooky feeling that you think about a subject and your hair seems to stand on end, and you get excited.

I don't think that you can really judge your contemporaries. There's absolutely too much emphasis on giving people A's, B's, C's and D's. If the world has not been blown up in the next few weeks because of the idiocies of George W. Bush, who thinks you solve problems by nuking people – if we're all still around in 200 years from now, maybe somebody will be able to say which plays of Tennessee Williams were the best. But we're too close to it now. It may take years of the plays being performed – with new generations discovering them and new directors directing them – and then we might have an idea which was the best and which was the least interesting.

With most really great artists, even their failures are interesting. Go to see *Titus Andronicus* by William Shakespeare. Even if it's not quite your cup of tea, there's something in it that's interesting, because it's Shakespeare. It may not be as good as *Hamlet* or as good as *Romeo and Juliet*, but it's still of interest. I think this whole insanity of grading artists is a kind of hangover from people's school days.

We writers don't choose our material – the material chooses us. The stupidest thing about critics is that they are forever saying, "Why did so and so write about that unworthy subject?" As if we could choose what we were going to write about.

Shakespeare had all these Italian plots to draw on. So why would he write a long, perplexing play about a prince whose father is murdered by his uncle, then his uncle marries his mother? If you had gone to Shakespeare and said, "You're working out your Oedipal problems," you would have made it impossible for him to write *Hamlet*.

People are drawn to certain myths because they reflect certain internal questions that they are asking themselves – conflicts they cannot even describe in words. They are drawn to them for reasons they don't understand.

Only when the work is completed, can the artist even think, "Maybe I was drawn to that material because…" But that's usually way after the fact.

It's that excitement, that kind of shivering feeling, that something moves you. That weirdly spooky feeling that you think about a subject and your hair seems to stand on end, and you get excited. And you don't really know why. You're only going to know after you've completed the work.

Sometimes I open *Entertainment Weekly* and a movie will be reviewed, and it will say, "This movie gets a C+." What kind of absurd, infantile way is that of reacting to a work of art? I totally disapprove of that. I thought, for example, that Steven Spielberg's movie, *Munich*, was absolutely fascinating because he did not have villains and heroes. He had characters on both sides that were so polluted by the practice of violence that their lives were ruined by violence. It didn't matter whether they were Israelis or Palestinians. There were many shades of gray.

I don't know about the response overseas, but when the movie opened in the United States, people absolutely hated Spielberg for it. What they were reacting against was their view of him as the hero of the Jews after *Schindler's List*, and now he dared to make a movie about the Palestinian–Israeli conflict in which the characters were not definite heroes and not definite villains. People got very angry with that, because it didn't suit their simplistic view.

There are some people who understand what criticism means, but most of them do not write for newspapers or magazines. Criticism should be helping spectators or readers to understand something better, not grading it A, B, C, or D. Criticism should be elucidating. But that kind of criticism really is very, very rare.

Creative people I admire

There are many works in the arts that I particularly admire. Spielberg is one who I feel has really grown as an artist. I very much admire Doris Lessing, who has grown and written many dozens of books but has never been nominated for a Nobel prize, probably because she is a woman. She grew up in Rhodesia, now Zimbabwe, and has written autobiographies, science fiction novels, contemporary novels and short stories. And she has written beautifully about the race issues in Africa. She's an incredible world figure.

Let me go back to Mozart again – he's one of my great favorites. Had anyone spoken to him when he was writing *The Magic Flute* or *Don Giovanni*, I don't think he would have said anything even remotely similar to what later commentators say about those operas.

He might have said, "Well, I found this interesting story by Lorenzo Da Ponte, and I'm going to see what I can do with it. It's about this guy, Don Giovanni, who seduces all the women in Spain. Don Giovanni's sidekick, named Laparello, keeps a list of all the women he has seduced. Eventually, all this catches up with him. A talking statue tells him that he is damned and he winds up in hell. Let's see if anything will come of it." That's the attitude of the working artist.

Julie Taymor, another one of my favorites, did an amazing job with the new production of Mozart's *The Magic Flute*. What Julie did was to take all the Masonic stuff, which is usually very perplexing, and make it clear. By creating enlarged images – puppets and diaphanous wings and mythological creatures – it gave new meaning to the story of the opera. I thought it was wonderful, but it was not traditional enough opera for some of the critics. That's the price you often pay for trying to do anything creative.

I started as a poet and I'm still a poet, and I read many poets' works with great pleasure. I couldn't even tell you who my favorite is, because there are so many wonderful poets. For one, I love the Polish poet Wyslawa Szymborska. She won a Nobel prize and is really good. She writes in Polish and I only read her in translation, but she's great even in translation.

Like other writers, I have many books where, after writing one or two hundred pages, I couldn't believe in the occasion of the book anymore – the premise of the book or the main characters. And I just put it aside. You put stuff aside, sometimes because it really doesn't work, or sometimes because you're just not yet ready to write it.

But what often happens is that some character will emerge from these pages later on and give me a different start in a different way. Sometimes that happens and sometimes it never happens.

I don't really think when I'm working of the effect of my work. It's only after the fact that people tell me things. I never think, "Oh, this book will have such and such an effect on so and so." I'm completely consumed in the task of writing it. And some of my books have been beloved, big best-sellers and some have sold not as well. But I never think of that when I'm working. I only think of the task I've set myself and how I can fulfill it.

Later, people may come to me and say, "You saved my life. You made me feel less like a freak. You helped me to understand myself better. You inspired me."

I do believe that I've opened a door for many people by writing honestly about feelings. And other writers will build on that.

JULIE TAYMOR

Moving, touching, entertaining and inspiring people

Julie Taymor is the critically acclaimed director of Broadway shows, films and opera. Her studies of mythology and folklore at Oberlin College in Ohio, her attendance at L'École Internationale de Théâtre Jacques Lecoq, and her early exposure to Asian theater in Sri Lanka, India and Japan led to her fascination with puppetry and experimental theater. Her Broadway adaptation of the Disney film The Lion King *earned her two Tony Awards and made her name a household word. This success was followed by directing several plays, including* Titus Andronicus *by Shakespeare and the film adaptation* Titus, *the film* Frida *about the Mexican painter Frida Kahlo, and opera productions such as Mozart's* The Magic Flute *and* Grendel, *a new modern opera.*

It's within human nature to be creative – it's what we do. Starting from birth, to talk, to put forward ideas and to communicate – all these are creative acts.

When you use creativity in the arts, in words or in music, you do so because you want to go beyond the norm, beyond what's necessary. You want to make more things happen in the world than need to happen. Or perhaps you need it for your own spirit.

When you talk about creating children, or food for survival – those are things that are necessary. But if you want to create a magnificent meal with extra-ordinary spices, or put together culinary components that you had never thought of before – that is being creative. It's beyond the necessary. It's not for health reasons or any specific requirement, but it's necessary for your spiritual well-being.

As for me, creativity is not something I sought out – it's just part of the fabric of who I am. You cannot *learn* to be creative. It has to be part of you. You can learn how to be more technically proficient, or how to gain skills relating to the arts. But the creative act itself, or the desire to be creative, is not something you can learn or acquire. You cannot make it happen. It is there because it just has to be.

Why are some people born to be clever stockbrokers, or born to be successful economists, while others are born to be great dancers and artists? I don't know

Julie Taymor. *Photo: Brigitte Lacombe*

the answer to that and I don't know anyone who has the answer to that. I can only speak more specifically about how I create projects, how I get ideas and how I carry these ideas forward.

What motivates me, above all, is that I enjoy it. I enjoy telling stories and I have a need to tell those stories. I enjoy putting the pieces of the stories together with other artists and collaborators. I love affecting people with the performances or the films that I direct. I have something I want to say to them, and I have the ability to pull it off.

> Being able to touch people and transform their lives in some way is very gratifying to me.

My gratification comes from thinking up a story, collaborating, creating the means to communicate the story, and having an audience – spectators who have been moved, viscerally, intellectually, or even politically and socially. Being able to touch people and transform their lives in some way is very gratifying to me.

When we talk about people who are creative, we often think of architects, artists, composers, or scientists, because they take you to a place – beyond the mundane, everyday basic state – to which you wouldn't necessarily go.

And, if you're successful doing this, you get paid for it and then that's what you do to survive. Thank goodness, I don't have to work in a restaurant or a bank, because I can actually make a living by doing the creative things that I love.

My work is my sustenance, and I'm not a nine to five person. I'm not an "Okay, now I go home from the office and I am free" kind of a person. If you're doing what I do, you're living with your work pretty much twenty-four hours of the day. I live it. It's an inseparable part of me. I'm never free from the things that I'm involved in. They are always there until I finish them, and then, hopefully, I move on to the next project.

That doesn't mean that all I do is work, work, work. I love to take vacations, ski and travel, and would consider these as my favorite pastimes. Occasional relaxation is my way of gathering inspiration for whatever my next project may be.

Getting inspiration

My inspirations come from numerous places. To begin with, I had parents who gave me a lot of freedom to act upon my desires to try things out. Although my family were not practitioners in the arts, they were very much lovers of the arts. They talked about it a lot and as a child I already had a tremendous opportunity to see theater and music and dance.

My father was a doctor. My mother was in politics, as was my sister. My brother started as a musician but now he is a doctor. So both my siblings followed more in my parents' footsteps – while I went halfway around the world and into the arts. But they were always encouraging.

Travel has always been a major inspiration for me. At the very young age of fifteen, I went to India and Sri Lanka as part of the Experiment in International Living program. I then went to Paris where I studied with Jacques Lecoq at the L'École Internationale de Théâtre Jacques Lecoq.

When, later on, I went to Oberlin College, I majored in folklore mythology. I studied world mythologies and religions in the course of studying anthropology, which was more than theater and the arts. That was my foundation and my jumping off point. Having a strong base in understanding world mythologies, together with my other experiences, would play a major part in my future career.

After I graduated from Oberlin, I did a Watson Fellowship that brought me to Indonesia and Japan and Eastern Europe. This was a wonderful opportunity for studying what I was interested in – experimental theater, puppet theater and visual theater.

Of course, there were always other inspirations – such as my favorite film-makers or favorite theater directors. But being creative does not specifically come from any outside influence. It comes from within. It's something that just happens to be there, deep inside of you, from the beginning.

> ... being creative does not specifically come from any outside influence. It comes from within.

I started to be creative at a very young age and was actually putting on dramas when I was only seven. I had a closet full of old clothes and I would put on plays in the garage and in our backyard and tell stories together with my brother and sister. And I've been doing theater since I was eleven.

This was not because I was seeking it out. It just came to me. I never really studied the craft very well and I've always been more of a practitioner than a student. The student part was my travel and watching other theater companies and other directors in the world, whether it was in Japan, or Indonesia, or Mexico.

Travel always inspired me because I've always been curious. I love going to places where I've never been. I love the idea of stretching my horizons, and thinking in ways I'm not used to thinking. Asia, in particular, has always been interesting to me because the theater in Asia has one of the strongest living traditions anywhere – it is continuously living and still very potent today.

At the time I lived in Indonesia, there was not much television or film. Theater was the dominant entertainment and art form and it was an integral part of the everyday life of their society. And that was very inspiring to me.

Scene from *The Lion King* with director/designer Julie Taymor's giraffe creations of actors on four stilts. *Photo: Joan Marcus*

Starting with a dream

It's hard to say how creative ideas come into your head. I doubt that anybody who is creative could tell you exactly how that happens.

My ideas sometimes come in dreams. Other times, they may come while I'm talking with someone about something. A lot of times an idea comes to me in the middle of a discussion about a project and I'll go, "Oh, wait a second. I know how to do that. What if we try this?"

I am an observer. My inspirations often come from what I see and hear from outside. That way I get a lot of ideas and then put them together. I like moving from one medium to another – from theater, to opera, to musicals, to films. I don't like one media more than the other and I don't like to be classified as leaning more to one than the other. I'm a painter and a sculptor, and make masks and puppets and costume design. All of that is fun for me. I love the variety because I really loathe boundaries.

Getting ideas often depends upon what I'm doing. I wear a number of creative hats. As a sculptor or as a director – each kind of job has a different process. Sometimes I may sketch a character out in pencil or I may sculpt the features in clay.

Sculpting is one of those gifts that came to me naturally. I've been sculpting since I was a child. I never went to art school, but I was given tools to sculpt and paint, and that was how I got started – just doing it.

I love to sculpt. When I am sculpting a mask, it is just between me and my hands and my tools and the clay and I'm having a dialogue with the clay. The figure starts to evolve and it's one-on-one.

But when I'm directing people, it's a different story. Then I'm a psychiatrist, a psychologist and a choreographer, trying to find ways of eliciting the perform-ance out of someone else. I have to be creative in the process of rehearsing. That can be a very complicated role because it is not just one-on-one – it's you and the performer and a whole room full of people.

Then there is the time pressure. As a director in film or theater, you have all these extraneous pressures that sometimes help, and sometimes get in the way of creativity. It's very different from sitting home at my computer, conceiving and writing out ideas for a screenplay or a musical. Those I can do on my own at home, or from a dream, or with my other collaborators.

Sometimes, there are surprises. Someone may suggest something that doesn't seem very interesting at first, but then you have a turn of events and an idea pops into your head that seems to make lots of sense. And you start to feel that it was meant to be that way.

Different stories or different notions for a drama come from vastly different places. For example, I didn't seek to do *Spiderman*, the musical. When I was approached to do it, it was of marginal interest to me. But when I looked at the comic book material, I hit upon an idea that just came to me – a real revelation, an incredible idea that inspired me to do the project. Perhaps this idea came from a little comic book, but it resonated in the mythology that I'm very familiar with. And it buried inside me and it said, "This is the way to do it. And if you don't do it this way, don't bother doing the project."

I fastened on that, and even though I had to struggle to get some of the people who own the rights to it to go along with it, I hung onto that idea because it was so inspiring. The next step was to go out and make sure the idea would work.

I never have any particular criteria for doing a film or a theater piece. Each story, each theme and each project is different. Some stories may have similar themes, but they can still be different in some ways. But unless I really feel that it's a story worth pursuing and telling, I won't be interested in spending time on it.

I'm a drama maker and so, to begin with, anything I do has to have a theme and a dramatic story. Since doing a project eats up such an enormous amount of time, I have to be able to fall in love with it. I never get into a project half-heartedly. It has to be something that I believe in 100 percent. If I'm not convinced of that, I'd rather not do it.

The process of creating

One of the most fascinating projects I ever did was the opera *Grendel*. Both Elliot Goldenthal, my partner and the composer of the opera, and I had separately read John Gardner's novel, *Grendel*, before we ever met. I had also read the *Beowulf* epic and did a comparative study of the epic and the novel when I was in college.

Like Edgar Allan Poe's short story of the outsider dwarf, or Horacio Quiroga's *Juan Darien* – the story of the jaguar that becomes a boy and is persecuted and killed – the monster's point of view in the story of *Grendel* appealed to me as a wonderful story to tell to people. Since the story dealt with an outcast from society, I wanted to have people who see the opera step outside their own shoes, and look at their own society and their own condition with a different set of eyes.

> It's my belief that an artist should give people new glasses and a new cubistic approach to looking at themselves

It's my belief that an artist should give people new glasses and a new cubistic approach to looking at themselves, so that they see themselves not in the mirror, but from behind their heads. By doing that, you hopefully widen someone's experience of living.

So when you take a novel like *Grendel* or the *Beowulf* legend, what should it be? A play? A movie? A musical? An opera? When I met Elliot, we discussed the story and decided that we wanted to do it as a large-scale grand opera. This was many years ago. We then had to start to visualize various aspects: How do you tell the story, in what kind of environment, for what scale theater? What means would best communicate the story – dance, music or chorus? Who should be the principal players?

Puppets in Julie Taymor's staging of *The Magic Flute. Photo: Ken Howard*

I began breaking down the story and writing the basic libretto and the scenario. I had to conceive the whole thing in my head, and then respond to the composer's work. And, in this case, I brought in another librettist, Sandy McClatchy, who is a poet, to help refine the script and the language.

We then had to go to several opera houses, and say, "Are you interested in commissioning this?" Nigel Redden, the director of the Lincoln Center Festival, had been interested in it for quite a while. The Los Angeles Opera, where I had staged another opera – Wagner's *The Flying Dutchman* – was also very interested. Eventually, the money was raised to commission the work. Now we had to seriously get to work on staging it. It took three years to complete it.

I did several other classical music productions, such as Mozart's *The Magic Flute* and Stravinsky's *Oedipus Rex*. I had done *The Magic Flute* in Florence at the Maggio Musicale for Zubin Mehta. After that, the Metropolitan Opera in

New York thought that my production of *The Magic Flute* would be a good season opening night program.

Another project on which Elliot Goldenthal and I collaborated was the film *Frida*, the story of the Mexican painter, Frida Kahlo, whose bout with polio as a young child – and a bus accident that injured and horribly disfigured her – did not prevent her from doing a lot of paintings.

I really didn't know much about her until I was offered the job of directing the film. Her paintings were loved by some people, but not by everybody. More than anything else, I found the unusual and turbulent love affair between Diego Rivera and Frida Kahlo the real reason to do the film.

Frida was a really great character to explore and a tremendous subject for a film. Learning about her life and her hardships was inspirational and her environment of Mexican folk art and customs such as the ceremonies associated with the "Day of the Dead celebrations" made a profound impression on me.

You have to separate being attracted to a story that you want to make into a film, and having the persons themselves affecting your life. That's what I had to do with this film. Even though I initially knew nothing about Frida Kahlo and I didn't particularly like her artwork, her life story so fascinated me that I decided that it was a good subject for me to do.

Another good story for me was the musical *The Lion King*. I thought it would be an interesting challenge to try and bring what was a successful animated film into a theatrical milieu, using different rules and regulations and using theatrical devices to tell a story that was done so differently in cinema.

> ... art is not just what you find in museums.

Different stories have different reasons to be taken into a medium. Different ideas about a project are the things that turn you on to making it into a play, opera, or film. You need to evaluate different aspects of a story, the possibilities of theatricalizing it or making it cinematic. You have to ask yourself, "Would that story be wonderful to put on film and how would I do it?"

I've done a number of things where I go from theater to film. *Titus Andronicus*, for instance, was a Shakespeare play that I did one way in the theater and then thought that it would make a spectacular film. So I had a good time doing the adaptation.

But to do this, I had to make a lot of critical decisions: How do I take what is really a play in verse and put it into a cinematic medium that has to be literal, that's in locations and that you feel is like living flesh and blood? How can you make sure that it's not so stylized that you don't believe in its reality and yet, at the same time, keep the theatrical nature of the material?

What I adored about doing *Titus* was the draw between the reality and the surrealism, the exquisite beauty of the language, and the horrifying nature of the story that seemed so real to me. Much more than *Hamlet* or any of the other more refined Shakespeare works, *Titus Andronicus* seemed more honest, more direct and contemporary. All those reasons – the subject matter, the art, the theatrical nature of the material, the language and the politics – made me want to make it into a film.

My aspiration

It is amazing how much art affects us socially in this country. Of course, the definition of art may differ from person to person. In my mind, art is not just what you find in museums. Clothing and fashion are art and not just a covering on your body to keep you from the cold. What you put on your T-shirts is art. You may think it is bad art but, with millions of people wearing T-shirts with all sorts of graphics, it certainly has affected a lot of people all over the world.

Even television is art. What is horrifying me is how bad a lot of television is, and how this affects people socially. But, as bad as it is, it is still art.

And, whether you like it or not, pop music and rock music are art. It's pop culture, but it's still art, sometimes for the good, and sometimes not so good. I, for one, love rock music and I'm working on two rock musicals. I feel that this is a powerful art medium and, if it's well done, it can be fun and inspiring for a lot of people.

I love what I am doing, but I realize that theater and films are ephemeral. An author's work or a poet's work lives on because it's written down. A composer's work lives on, because the score is on paper. But a director's work is ephemeral, because it's not on paper and so it doesn't live on. It's like a Navajo sand painting – it's there for a time and then it's gone.

Perhaps a few of my films may live on. If one of my films has as much resonance ten years from the time it is first shown, it may have relevance in people's lives that transcends generations. When people are moved by a film, concert, or theater piece, their lives are enriched.

My aspiration has been to inspire people. To have them think about the state they are in and move them, touch them, entertain them and inspire them. To make them think about what they're doing with their lives and what is happening around them. To transport them to another place for a moment or for two hours and give them a sense of wonder – of awe.

JAMES ROSENQUIST

Making an illusion on two-dimensional surfaces

James Rosenquist, the acclaimed American artist, has applied his experience of painting large billboards as a young man to his current creation of super-large canvases. By taking fragmented, unrelated images and combining these in provocative ways on his canvases, he has gained the reputation of being a leading pop artist. His many retrospectives include the Whitney Museum of American Art in New York and the Wallraf-Richartz Museum in Cologne, Germany. He is exhibited at the leading world galleries and museums, and receives large-scale commissions from around the world. His numerous awards include the Golden Plate Award from the American Academy of Achievements and the Fundación Cristóbal Gabarrón award in Spain.

There is really no clear definition of creativity.

Every creative person is different from the other, even if artists are linked together as groups with specific energies or styles. These groups are often given names by the art world, like abstract expressionism or Dadaism. However, the artists within these groups are usually so totally different from each other – different in thinking, in styles, in media and in everything else – that any definition of their creative activities sounds hollow. And, as time passes, these definitions mean less and less.

So, how can you define a creative person? Young artists often ask me, "How do you get ideas? How do you do it?" When they ask me this, I say, "Look back to your childhood. Has anything strange or very unusual ever happened to you that you couldn't figure out, and you wanted to think about it and talk about it? That's how ideas often start."

Growing up poor

I grew up during the Great Depression in North Dakota, in the country out on the prairie, and that had a definite influence on my life because of the idiosyncrasies of the economics at that time and life in general. We lived on a farm and we had nothing – no electricity, no telephone, no toys.

There were no iPods or MTV in those days – we didn't even have a radio.

James Rosenquist in Aripeka, Florida, 2006. *Photo: Beverley Coe*

Luckily, I had a tomboy aunt who used to entertain me by making marionettes, model airplanes and other toys. People innovated. I remember my grandfather taking a pair of old shoes, welding on some wood files to the bottom and grinding them down to make them into ice skates.

I grew up among an interesting family. At the time, I never thought that my family was interesting, but it turns out that they were very unusual. My mother was an aviator in 1931 and so was my father. They met at the Grand Forks, North Dakota airport. My mother never had a pilot's license, since this was before women's liberation and she never got one. But she flew all over the place, anyway. My uncle Albert was in the Army Air Corps. My father wanted to start "an international airline." To do this, uncle Albert and my father wanted to sell their cars, buy an airplane and get an airmail route between Grand Forks and Winnipeg, Canada. Unfortunately, Albert crashed and so their hopes were dashed.

> ... I grew up in an adventurous and inventive family, and that probably rubbed off on me.

As you can see, I grew up in an adventurous and inventive family, and that probably rubbed off on me.

Last year, I went out to North Dakota again, when I was awarded an honorary doctorate at the University of North Dakota. While there, I went searching for the town where I used to go for soda pop. It was totally erased. The Deaconess Hospital, where I was born, is now the Happy Dragon Chinese restaurant. The train tracks were torn up and the train station was taken down. The grain elevator was torn down. The general store no longer exists. The town was just wiped off the map. It was a little depressing, as if my childhood had just disappeared.

The beginning of the artist in me

In 1949 I won a scholarship for a watercolor, which paid for four Saturdays at the Minneapolis School of Art. Later, my mother said, "Jim, you're always drawing. You could make some money out of this."

One day, when I was a teenager, I saw an ad in the paper, "Wanted, artist sign painter." The ad was by someone named W.G. Fischer, a rough and tough guy who just got out of the army at the end of World War II. I went to see him and he gave me $100 and told me to go and paint "Philips' 66 Gasoline" signs on big gasoline storage tanks all through Minnesota, South Dakota, North Dakota, Wisconsin and Iowa. I had to do that all by myself and I did it really well.

Then, when I was nineteen, I applied for a job to paint pictures for General Outdoor Advertising in Minneapolis. After several tries, I got the job. So now I was a commercial artist and I was making more money than my father who had a job as an airplane inspector.

James Rosenquist working on *The Light That Won't Fail I*, Coenties Slip studio, New York, c. 1961.
Courtesy James Rosenquist Inc. Photo: Paul Berg

While planning to ride a motorcycle to California after high school, I started to take art courses at the University of Minnesota. There I met Cameron Booth, an art teacher. I knew how to draw, especially portraits, but Booth said to me, "There's nothing for you here. You should go to New York and study with Hans Hoffman." Booth had taught at the Art Students League in New York City in the 1940s, but then moved back to Minneapolis. He had taken a liking to me and gave me a lot of valuable advice. I think, without Cameron Booth, I probably would not be an artist today.

Hans Hoffman quit teaching in New York and moved to Provincetown. At the recommendation of Cameron Booth, I applied to the Art Students League

James Rosenquist working on *The Persistence of Electrical Nymphs in Space*, Aripeka studio, Florida, c. 1985. *Photo: Gianfranco Gorgoni*

and won one year's free schooling there. I studied at the Art Students League with some of the famous old teachers there at the time, like Edwin Dickinson, George Grosz, Morris Kantor and Will Barnet.

After leaving the Art Students League, I joined the International Sign Painters Union Local 230. That was in the old union days, when management was terrible, and you had to join a union to protect yourself. My fellow workers were largely Italian and, as I found out after I got to know them, some were old 1930's New York Communists.

My first job was in Brooklyn, painting "Hebrew National Salami" signs. This was very difficult because, like the Superman logo, the Hebrew National logo went back in space and I was not very good at lettering. I only lasted a month at that job.

I really was a picture painter and I could paint any kind of picture. So I got another job in Brooklyn with General Outdoor Advertising who sent me out to paint two-story Schenley whiskey bottles above every candy store. I wound up painting 140 of them. On the label, it said, "This spirit is made from the finest grains." After a while, I got so sick of it that I wrote, "Mary had a little lamb, its fleece was white as snow." That's probably the first notion of what people call pop art today. You really could not see it from the street, but when they took the sign down they saw it and they said, "We're going to get fired. What is this kid doing here?"

Then I graduated to Times Square to work for Artkraft Strauss. I was twenty-two years old and my helpers were between forty-five and seventy-five years old. Times Square was a different place in those days. The nature of my work was to go up to a big desk and select different images, assemble them all and scale them for big billboards in Times Square. This could be a tomato, a pack of cigarettes, movie stars, food, anything. I was supposed to scale these to fit at various locations, such as the Astor Victoria

> One thing you have to learn in this business is that you can't afford to have a bad first show

Theater, the Palace, or the Mayfair Theater. I became really good at scaling an image and proportioning it into one foot squares on the sign and then drawing in a face, or a cake, or beer, or whatever.

And that's really how I got started thinking in terms of very large surfaces.

But I had to work high up in the air. In 1959, when two of my fellow workers got killed falling off the scaffolding, I decided that this work was too dangerous for me and I quit.

I started thinking about what the world meant to me. At the suggestion of Ellsworth Kelly, I rented a loft for $45 a month and started putting together ideas that, at first, I thought were ridiculous. But that is how I got started painting the way I do today.

Becoming a professional painter

When I first came to New York, I had letters of introduction from Cameron Booth to many middle-aged artists who did abstract art. Most of them were doing commercial work because they couldn't sell their paintings. They had to make a living, so some did fashion for the *New York Times*, some worked for television and so on. They had cocktail parties to show each other their abstract art. But they couldn't sell any of it. There was no market for abstract art at the time.

You could count the contemporary collectors without taking your shoes off, there were so few of them. In time, some of these artists gathered steam and got to be known. They knew that they had to get better and better and have something really fantastic before they could have a one-man show.

In those days, rents in New York were cheap. I had a five-room apartment on the Upper East Side for $31 a month. Living in a cosmopolitan city like New York was great. You could live like a king because almost everything was free – the museums were free and so was most everything else.

Today, the young would-be artists have to deal with exorbitant rents – $3,000–4,000 a month. So they think that have to make money from their fine art immediately and they rush and rush to put something together to have a show.

> ... my creations try to be a question, rather than an answer.

One thing you have to learn in this business is that you can't afford to have a bad first show, both career wise and money wise. Most young artists don't have the money to carry on. Nobody is waiting for them. And if your first show crashes, you are out. To get your art career on the way, your first one-man show has to be a knockout.

On the road to success

Sometime, during World War II, I went into a museum in Ohio and I saw an exhibition consisting of three things – a little painting, a live flower and a shrunken head. And I wondered, "What in the world is that supposed to mean?" But this got me thinking about collage.

Now, my work is mostly from making collage that I dream up and then paint. Some people wonder where and when collage got started and they point often to Kurt Schwitters who was famous for collage at the beginning of the twentieth century. "Collage," a French word meaning "to join," describes the idea of putting different images together. This probably originated with the Japanese tea ceremony. On a table, the Japanese would put together various objects, like a painting, a flower and maybe a beautiful tea bowl. Combining several divergent images may not necessarily communicate a specific idea, but it is meant to bring forth a spark of intellectual thoughts.

That's the reason I believe that collage will remain a contemporary medium.

In February 1962, I had my first exhibition at a gallery called The Green Gallery on 57th Street in New York City and it was a sellout. The prices, at that time, were between $750 and $1,000. Some of these paintings have since been resold for several million dollars.

At that time, Dick Bellamy, my dealer, couldn't afford a secretary. So, to encourage a beautiful young girl to work for Bellamy, I gave her a little painting. It was just a little thing, about 10 × 18 inches. The young lady is probably about sixty years old now, but she hung on to the little painting. This past year, it was auctioned off for $350,000, and I hear that she received the money.

How ideas come to me

In my work today, peculiar ideas sometimes occur to me and I try to make a painting out of them. Usually, my creations try to be a question, rather than an answer. I am not trying to solve problems – I am trying to create dynamic pictorial inventions on a two-dimensional surface. The reason I don't do sculpture is because I believe that creating an illusion on a two-dimensional surface may be more difficult than making a three-dimensional sculpture.

By now, I've had many shows of my work. Among my shows in 2006 was a big one in London and in Switzerland at the Basel Art Fair. Soon I will have one with Ernst Beyeler, a wealthy art patron with a substantial collection of numerous works by Picasso, Nolde, Munch and other expressionists. In New York City, my work is being shown at Aquavella Galleries, a prestigious gallery on East 79th Street, where there is always a lot of action going on.

I tend to relate strongly to certain art periods and admire a lot of those artists. Some have probably influenced me in one way or another. I've learned a lot from Renaissance period artists and the Golden Mean Rectangle. For an interesting picture plane, I look at Cubists. For color, I look at French Impressionists. These artists have contributed so much to what we do today.

One of the contemporary artists I admire is Robert Rauschenberg. He has a brilliant mind. He's over eighty-one years old now and in a wheelchair, but he's still sharp as a tack so far as his mind goes. Barnett Newman, the abstract expressionist, was a good friend of mine. I also knew Franz Klein and Bill de Kooning, both great artists. All of them have made a deep impression on me.

Another artist I admire is Menasha Kadishman, the Israeli sculptor. I met him on several occasions when I went to Israel. In 1980, I went there on behalf of the US Information Service. I like the people in Israel – you have to hand it to them – they have such a great spirit in the face of many problems. But they need to realize that suffering does not ensure great art. Some of their sculptures look like gun emplacements.

> I'm always trying to do things that no one has ever seen before

Anywhere I go, I look for someone who pushes the boundaries out further and further, someone who has great ideas and knows how to communicate these through art. Occasionally I see it, but most of the time I don't.

Getting ideas

For me, ideas come through all sorts of visual impressions. For instance, one day, at an amusement park in Texas, I saw a rusting B-36 bomber. Afterwards, I did a painting called *F-111*. It showed a fighter-bomber being built.

James Rosenquist working on *F-111*, Broome Street studio, New York, c. 1964. *Courtesy James Rosenquist Inc. Photo: Hans Namuth*

It had not flown yet but, to me, it was already an obsolete war weapon. Building them kept Americans busy and having two-and-a-half children and three-and-a-half cars. So the economy of the United States was thriving. I thought: Why are all these big chunks of killer weapons being made as a threat if they are never actually used? It was the Cold War, but to me all this was totally ridiculous.

This 86-ft. long *F-111* painting showed a little girl under a hair dryer. With this I meant to represent the pilot of a full-sized bomber flying through the flack of the economy. The painting was criticized at the time for being antiwar, which it was. But many other ideas motivated me, such as peripheral vision.

I eventually sold the painting for $25,000. A couple of years ago, the Museum of Modern Art bought it from the third owner for $5,000,000. This sort of disproportionate transaction would bother some artists, but it doesn't bother me. I was happy to get $25,000 at that time.

I'm always trying to do things that no one has ever seen before in color and form. I'm doing abstract painting where shapes and forms seem to be evolving while you are looking at the painting. In other words, just when you think you can identify something, it is changing right in front of your eyes. This is done on a two-dimensional canvas with no sound effects or music or anything else. To achieve it, I make many, many sketches, select the best of the sketches and have my men prepare canvasses. Then I start painting.

I can paint anything as long as I have a sketch to work from. So it's up to me to develop something that I think works well in an 8 × 10-inch size. Then I can paint any size painting from that. I can paint huge areas. I've done six 17 × 46-ft. paintings.

I even did a 133 × 24-ft. painting for the French government eight years ago to celebrate the fiftieth anniversary of Eleanor Roosevelt signing the Declaration of Human Rights. But while I was working on it, France changed ministers of culture. As a result, they never took it or paid for it. But the Swiss wanted to show it and it was exhibited in Basel. They didn't buy it either, but I have a couple of nibbles from other sources to buy the work.

Ideas for abstract paintings come to me from trying to do something I've never seen before and that I've never seen anyone else do before. I start painting only when I'm convinced that I actually have a good idea.

Then, after I finish a painting, someone comes along and says, "I like that. I would like to buy it." Then another person comes and says, "I like that. I want to buy it." Eventually, a third person wants to buy the painting. If you have three people, then you have a market.

With commissioned work, it is another situation and I occasionally work on commission. The Rockefellers asked me to do a long painting for the new subway station at Rockefeller Center in New York City. The idea was to do something about New York City. So I asked fifty people, "What does New York mean to you?" I asked some old friends in Brooklyn, and they said to me, "Jimmy, you put the poor people on the left, the rich people on the right and the struggle in the middle." I said, "I know that."

But my real definition for New York City is that it is a place where anybody from anywhere can come and be as successful as they want to be – if they are lucky! I've known some fantastic people who came to New York and became famous. I've also met some fabulously talented people who came and just faded away.

Unexpected results

Occasionally, a painting comes out in a very unexpected way. You start it, you are into it, and then something happens so that it evolves into something you just did not expect.

Let's say I am making a huge, 17 × 46-ft. picture. After doing some sketches, I start working on the painting. I feel like an ant crawling up hill. I am working and working and as I get it about 70 percent finished, I suddenly realize that I could have gone much further. I begin to see things that I could have done that would have extended this concept into something much more brilliant.

I then have to try that idea on another painting, because it would be difficult erasing thousands of square feet of paint.

Sometimes, ideas also come to me from unexpected directions. For instance, I once learned that Albert Einstein, the great thinker, said that the traveler and the spectator seeing the same thing at the speed of light see it differently.

So, with Einstein's theory in mind, I started doing a series, called *Speed of Light* paintings. I did one 17 × 46 footer called *The Stowaway Peers Out at the Speed of Light* and a number of other speed of light pictures, where I tried to show that what you are looking at is not what is on the canvas. What's beneath the paint is the archeology of all my experience.

Learning how to do it

With two scholarships and meeting Cameron Booth and the Union painting experience, I've been very lucky. I now have seven honorary doctorates and have given talks in probably over a hundred universities and colleges, where I see art departments and teachers who talk about a lot of things but don't really know how to teach the students to become artists.

Instead of subjecting the students to "one from column A and one from column B," it would be better if, at some point, they put their students in isolation chambers and ask them to think about their whole makeup as a human beings, with blood running through their bodies, and who they are.

Then I would give them a historical education in Europe. By being around art all the time, art means a great deal to Europeans. I could be walking down the street in Trieste, Italy, and a window would open three stories up, and someone would shout "Hey, Rosenquisto, buon giorno!" A guy would come down with a glass of wine, take me up to his kitchen and on his refrigerator is an image of one of my paintings.

James Rosenqist working on *Through the Eye of the Needle to the Anvil*, Aripeka studio, Florida, c. 1988.
Courtesy James Rosenquist Inc.

In the United States, there is a small audience for the arts, although it is growing. Unfortunately, there is very little money from the National Endowment for the Arts. Also, neither art nor music is taught any longer in most schools. Or, if it is taught, it's usually the lowest priority. It's a shame.

When I had my show at the Guggenheim Museum, I gave three lectures on how to get the paint out of the tube on the canvas in the right place. Only physical – no aesthetics, just "this is how you do it." That's what's really lacking in many universities, because they don't really understand how to do it.

My first lecture at the Guggenheim was how to set up a studio with no money, because many young artists don't have any money. How to go to the gas station and get a barrel to use for brush cleaning. How to just get the necessary tools to become a professional. Remember, this is not grade school – this is about teaching to be a professional.

The second lecture was about color, about which some teachers know very little. For instance, instead of using black paint, how to make black out of analogous or complementary colors to obtain analogously beautiful color relationships.

The third lecture was how to scale things up from a small sketch if you really want to do a large painting with accuracy. It's unfortunate that, most times, university and college students don't learn about those sorts of things.

If you want to be a painter, you have to know these things.

Developing to be your own person

Some people think that there are a number of artists who actually just copy my work, or try to copy my work. I guess that is a compliment. Every artist starts by copying other artists. Even Picasso copied Velasquez and other great artists. In time, good artists go on to develop their own style.

But when I see some young artists actually copying other artists, then I say they are not being themselves. They're simply creating replicas of other artists and, to me, that's not being creative.

When they were teenagers, I can just imagine their mothers saying, "Look, look in that magazine. Why don't you do something like that? Maybe you could sell it." Who knows – it might even be one of my paintings they're looking at.

I had to work hard to be where I am today. When I was fifteen years old, I was driving a truck. There was nothing else to do. But whenever I felt that I could do something creative, I was voracious. I would work, and work and work at it.

Having developed a personal style of my own, everything I do now is done in the scaling technique, a grid technique that I first learned as a sign painter.

Today, I have two giant studios – you could park four 737s in them – so that

I've been able to handle commissions for very large works, such as the Deutsche Guggenheim Museum in Berlin.

I consider myself very lucky. I am reasonably successful and lead a good life. Much of the time, I live and work at my studio on the Gulf of Mexico and when I get tired and covered with paint, I go out in my boat and jump in the Gulf and swim with the porpoises.

Even though I am getting older, I keep getting busier and busier. I hope that I can keep it up.

STEVE WOZNIAK

Inventing to simplify things

Steve Wozniak co-founded Apple Computer with Steve Jobs in 1976. He is considered the inventor of the personal computer, having created the Apple I and Apple II computers in the mid-1970s. With an engineering background and a mind for discovery, Wozniak and Apple Computer have helped transform our world. Steve has also been a major investor and concert promoter with the US Festivals and a philanthropist. He also spent a decade teaching fifth graders. He was inducted into the National Inventors Hall of Fame and has received numerous awards, including the National Medal of Technology and the Heinz Award.

I look back and wonder, "Why did I never want to accept things the way they were?"

I went to school and learned many techniques of doing things, but I always tried to think up new ways to do these things. My creativity came from two sources – my shyness and my love of computers.

I was very shy, and in my shyness I didn't want to just go out and do a job that a lot of other people could do. I wanted to look for ways in which I did not have to be competitive. I wanted to look for an approach that other people weren't doing, and so I tried to be different.

Secondly, I have loved computers ever since I was in elementary school, and in high school I worked very, very hard on computer designs with pencil and paper. I would try a little game of figuring out techniques of designing them to work with fewer computer chips. And I became excellent at that, because I did it weekend after weekend, just trying to think of ideas no one had ever thought of before, such as using a chip for something other than what it was intended for. That way, I came up with some very unique solutions.

My creative youth with electronics

The first thing you do when you're a kid engaged in electronics is take your gifts and electronic kits and build this and hook that together and have fun. But you

Steve Wozniak. *Courtesy of Margaret Wozniak*

aren't fully creative until you start thinking, "I want to do something special with these talents." That happened to me with building my own science fair projects. With the assistance and guidance of my father, I took weeks to build huge projects with hundreds of switches, lights, and wires. I also once built a model of the atom showing all the electron orbits. It was a pretty simple design and I was about nine years old.

And when I was ten, I built a tic-tac-toe "computer" out of logic. I had played every possible game of tic-tac-toe and I wrote down rules. I numbered the squares 1 to 9, and my rules were: if Xs are in 1 and 3, and nothing is in 2, then you take 2. I was really designing the machine myself, because I developed different sets of rules and still played the game of tic-tac-toe. I was trying to find five rules and shrink them all into one and say, "If this and that is true, then I'll go here." I wanted to be creative and make choices that other people wouldn't have made.

Then I built an adding-subtracting machine. I had seen designs for an adder made out of logic and a subtracter made out of logic, and I realized they were rather similar. So I worked and worked at it and drew in some extra gates of my own, and I made it so it could both add and subtract with very little change in the circuits. That was definitely creative. I was now designing and not just copying a design that already existed. And if something didn't work, I figured out what the problem was and how to fix it all on my own.

At that time I was about 12 years old.

My parents strongly influenced my values in life, but also whenever I needed help, or I wanted to learn something in electronics, my father was there to explain how things worked. By the time I went to high school I was really on my own.

My love affair with computers

We didn't have computers at our school, but my electronics teacher helped me get a job programming computers at a local company where I found a book called *The Small Computer Handbook*. I was always too shy to ask about computers and here was a book that described a computer. Wow – it was the highlight of my life!

I sat down alone, closed the door, took out some chip manuals, and I started trying to design little diagrams with pencil on paper – trying to make these chips add up to be a computer. I really think being self-taught is the best way, because many people teach outmoded methods. So for my last year of high school, I pretty much designed computer after computer.

I was designing computers but couldn't show them off to any teachers or kids, since they wouldn't know what they were. I didn't share them with anyone – not even my dad.

At the time, I didn't think I would ever design computers as an actual job, although minicomputers were coming out from Hewlett-Packard (HP), Digital Equipment, and others. I did it for fun. My motivation was inside me. The reason I wanted to get so good at this little game was just because it made me feel like I was winner. I didn't think I would get a salary, or a title, or awards, or yachts for doing it. I would just be pleased that I was doing the thing that I loved to do, which was designing computers.

> I didn't think I would get a salary, or a title, or awards, or yachts for doing it. I would just be pleased that I was doing the thing that I loved to do, which was designing computers.

And I played a game of, "How can I design it better and better, with fewer and fewer parts?" I developed some incredible skills that eventually led to a job in designing the hot product of the time – the scientific calculator at HP. And I didn't even have a college degree.

I just loved how computers worked and wanted my own computer. During my last year of high school, I told my dad that I was going to have a computer one day that could run a program. When he said it would cost as much as a house, I told him, "Well, then I'll live in an apartment." In other words, I wanted a computer rather than a house. That was my choice.

I was very much inspired by a club of people that also wanted their own computers. I was too shy to ever talk in the club or raise my hand, but I listened to all their words, and they were talking about social revolutions, and people who knew how to program computers being more important than CEOs.

Our computer club would discuss how people were going to become masters of solving their own problems once everyone could afford a computer in their home. The people in the club spoke from a technical point of view. It inspired me, because we used the word "revolution."

> I always wanted to be part of a revolution. It was part of my nature to not just follow authority.

I always wanted to be part of a revolution. It was part of my nature to not just follow authority. I was kind of rebellious and revolution was the right word for my way of thinking. I knew in my head, as these other people did, that the prices of certain chips, starting with the microprocessor, were going to make these machines affordable. And we weren't even looking into the future for prices to drop. We were looking at it as of that day.

I wanted to dedicate my design skills to helping the world get to this better social place. And not do it for a company or for money.

I actually gave my schematics away. I gave away the listings at first and helped other people wire up their own computers. I just wanted people to see that there was a formula that lets you build a computer that did what you needed at an affordable price.

I was goal directed and wanted to shun the ways of the past, because I knew that they were long, awkward and they wouldn't get me there, and I always thought that that's how computers had been built for forty years. But what about building one at an affordable price that works the way people want it to work?

Looking to simplify things

To build an affordable computer, I would think, "How might it be done in the world?" And I would try to look for clues, perhaps something in a book. We didn't have the internet back then. I'd look at parts that were available and wonder how to combine them in a way that will give me what I'm trying to build. If the combined parts were numerous, I'd always throw it away. Everything had to be very tiny, short and simple. Looking to simplify things was one of my great elements of creativity.

There are a lot of engineers who aren't inventors. Inventors want to think of new ideas and build them. They want to do it in their spare time. It's their love in life and their internal passion. Trying to pursue excellence and trying to be the best in the world is a part of it. And that just comes to some of us. Inventors tend to want to work on their own. They're loners. They want to have an idea, go into the lab, hook some things up, prove it out – and not say, "Oh, I have this idea, will you guys help me out? I'll do this part, you do that part." I had ideas, designed them, put the chips on boards, wired them together, wrote the software and did the hardware. I didn't ever have to interface with anyone. That's why my projects were also very fast.

> I just want to have something different that I choose to do, which I believe is right and solves the problem for the reasons I have.

I prefer to work in areas of electronics that are more unique, because then I avoid competition, where other people might say, "No, you should do it this way. You should use this kind of a chip." I never wanted to get into that whole competition thing. I just want to have something different that I choose to do, which I believe is right and solves the problem for the reasons I have.

I also have no problem with thinking differently from others. I don't have to convince somebody that chips should work this or that way. Or this political thing is right or wrong. If in my head I believe it, that's all that matters to me. If

I believe I have a technology approach that's good and makes a worthwhile machine, that's all I need. Then I'm confident and happy and I'll proceed forward, and fortunately I have the skills to design these things.

Developing the personal computer

The first people looking for affordable computers were mostly lower level employees – technicians – who wanted to own a computer because their company always owned the computer they used. And if they had their own computer, these people were going to be big, and more important.

Partly because they weren't really high notch engineers as I was, many of them used common approaches and copied

Steve Wozniak at age 11 with his ham radio setup.
Courtesy of Margaret Wozniak

others' circuits. When Intel published a circuit, they copied the Intel circuit. And Intel hadn't thought out personal computers. All Intel thought out was how to put a bunch of chips around a microprocessor that turned it into the guts, which, if you plug in enough other things, becomes a computer.

The engineers also all used the simplest memory chips you can buy called "static memory." And yet, the first 4K *dynamic memory* chips came out that year, 1975, and they were the first chips that were lower in cost than static memory. They were the chips that were going to make a programmable computer affordable.

I was actually well ahead of the rest of the world in designing very small computers, since I had done it before. I thought at the time that the goal was a computer that would enable me to sit at a keyboard and type in a program. Did I really need to build an ugly computer with mainframes, boards, wires, teletypes and printers, or could I just create something simple to solve my problems?

I initially limited my problems to two, thinking that if you could create a couple of things for computers to do, you could probably do all the things for which businesses use computers. The first thing was games, which were fun, and something that computers were able to do in those early days. The second thing was programming for my work at HP. I wanted my own computer for programming, instead of sharing the computer with the other HP engineers. I wanted to use the absolute minimum set of chips and electronics to do that in an affordable fashion.

How I co-founded Apple Computer

Steve Jobs and I were in high school when we first met and we found that we had much in common. We talked about electronics, music and pranks. We became good friends and he later worked at Atari while I was at HP.

Before the real PC, what was soon to become the Apple, I was the only computer designer that used *dynamic memory*. Nobody wanted to use dynamic memory, because it required you to do some extra design work. You had to design what's called "refresh circuitry" to keep the memory from forgetting its data. But while it was extra design work, it saved chips. The dynamic memories were four times the memory, one-fourth the chips, with half the cost. So for me it was the way to go, but nobody else did it. All these computer kits that were claiming they were computers were just glorified microprocessors using static memories.

Steve Jobs convinced me that the two of us could start a company. He first suggested that we build a preprinted circuit part of the computer – called the PC board – for $20 and sell it for $40. I finally agreed and I got approval from HP, where I was working. Hewlett-Packard didn't want to get involved in the project.

Forming the company was kind of odd, because I originally designed the Apple I computer for myself and to give away to others.

Some weeks later, after Steve returned from a place he called "the apple orchard," he suggested the company name – Apple Computer – which sounded better and more creative than the technical names we had previously considered.

Soon after that, a local computer store, which had watched me demonstrate my machine, gave us an order for a hundred fully built computer boards. We were now into the big time – a $50,000 order – and we had no money. So we received thirty days' credit on the parts, built them in ten days and got paid cash when we delivered the computer boards to the store. And that's how we started the business.

I was 25 and Steve was 21 at the time.

I sometimes discover things as I design and work these things out. But I usually start out knowing that what I'm designing is what I'm going to get. I'll have thought it out for a long time and have a pretty good picture in my head before I commit it to paper with a pencil.

Within about three months after the business started, I designed the Apple II. It was a major improvement over the Apple I, designed with text, graphics

Steve Jobs and Steve Wozniak in 1975 prior to founding Apple Computer. *Courtesy of Margaret Wozniak*

and color from the system's memory. It was the first PC that could work with a keyboard, display, game paddles and sound – and it was affordable. And that was my first real computer from the ground up.

I wasn't sure that color would work with the Apple II. It was so different from the way color was done in the past. I was not a color TV expert. I just knew that I was putting out signals that looked very similar to color TV signals, and when it worked, it was one of those eureka moments! Steve Jobs and I realized that this was going to be really big.

At HP, the engineers were astounded, and thought it was incredible, because they could instantly see how you can program your entire screen to have color, graphics and animation.

We knew we had something so huge that Steve and I couldn't do it by ourselves. We started to get financing to build the Apple II. Steve, my family and friends talked me into leaving my job at HP. We then moved from working in Steve's house and my apartment to a little office in Cupertino, California.

We had competitors, but the Apple II started the PC revolution. Going from cassette tape data storage to floppy disk drive enabled us to even run business programs. Suddenly, in the late 1970s, we were selling 10,000 computers a month! Our initial public stock offering in 1980 made many millionaires in a single day.

My favorite electronics project

I did the design for the floppy disk drive in two weeks. My motivation for rushing was not only to get a floppy disk for the Apple II, but also to go to Las Vegas with our company to show off the floppy disk.

A smaller five-inch disk was being introduced to replace the earlier eight-inch drive, and Steve Jobs thought that this was the future and wanted to go with it. I had never worked with floppy disks and never taken a design course for such things. So I was starting right from scratch, which is often where the best things come from. I then studied Shugart's disk drive and, as I began to understand what its chips did, I pulled out chips, one by one, thinking, "This chip isn't necessary. That chip isn't necessary." I pulled almost twenty chips out of their design. I kept some wires that were needed and eliminated circuits, because I'm so much into simplicity, and cleaning things up, and having few parts.

> We knew we had something so huge that Steve and I couldn't do it by ourselves.

Then I just designed a very clever circuit that used only five chips where the normal circuit might be fifty chips. Five chips – none of them special at all, just cheap little one-dollar chips used in very clever ways that nobody ever thought of and I wound up with a working floppy disk design. When I studied competitors' designs, I realized that mine worked better. I was off with another big winner!

My later career

I don't have a lot of time for hobbies. But, when I have chance, I like to play some computer games, such as Game Boy. I did get involved in the early development of arcade games. I designed games for myself, and I even designed a game for Atari. Actually, the Apple II was the earliest game computer – it was almost designed as a game machine as well as a computer. I have always loved games, but now they've become way too complicated for me.

These days, I'm very, very busy with computer appearances and speeches. I do a lot of volunteer work and I'm on many boards. And often, instead of driving a car, I ride my light little Segway into town, or I play Segway polo on it.

For a while, I was a concert promoter for the US Festivals. In 1982, we were the first to combine music and technology, using a huge video screen for the people in the back to view. The following year, we did another concert. Although I lost money on the concerts, they brought fun and laughter and were an important part of my life.

I also went back and I taught school for eight years – something I was going to do in my life without Apple – and I kept the press out of it. I had determined when I was in sixth grade that I wanted to become a fifth grade teacher. So I

Steve Wozniak in 1978 with the Apple II personal computer. *Courtesy of Margaret Wozniak*

taught computer skills to fifth graders here in Los Gatos, California. I also taught computer skills to sixth, seventh and eighth graders, and to teachers in our district. I became very busy, teaching up to seven days a week. I really always wanted to do that.

My keys to happiness

The most important thing in life is that you have to believe in yourself. If you have an idea and other people are saying, "No, no, that's not the way you do it" – well, don't just listen to others but try to think for yourself in order to get to the truth.

Perhaps people will think of me as a creative engineer who thought differently, who didn't mind going on different paths. My main goal has always been to build things that actually work and serve useful purposes at a very, very affordable price.

> If you have an idea and other people are saying, "No, no, that's not the way you do it" – well, don't just listen to others but try to think for yourself in order to get to the truth.

I think that PCs have done that by giving us more productivity. But I don't think they've necessarily given us more happiness. I believe they're just a point along this whole curve that humans move in order to get somewhere someday.

Basically, life's about how happy you are, and how much you laugh compared to how much you frown. It's not really about how much money you have or how many yachts you have. It's not how well you can manage and run companies and keep things working right in your house – it's really your happiness as a whole. You can have very little and yet be very happy and have a wonderful life.

ROLAND HEILER

Overruling the tendency to compromise

Roland Heiler, managing director and head of the Porsche Design Studio in Zell am See, Austria, started as an apprentice and, after holding several design positions with Porsche, is now responsible for supervising the design of Porsche Design that covers men's accessories, such as watches and eyewear, along with the design of electronic equipment, sports equipment and fashion – all upholding the uniform design signature of all products sold under the Porsche Design brand. The Studio also handles assignments in the areas of industrial and product design.

A s a designer, I tend to feel that the creative drive in a person is caused by the desire to step beyond existing boundaries. But the subject of creativity is very difficult to deal with as a single denominator.

The motivation to do something creative has to come from within. Some people are born with it, or they grow up in a way that they develop a desire to create things. I think that one thing that's typical of creative people is that they're very observant and always curious. They want to experiment with the unknown factors.

I believe that anybody who creates something is in some way or another not satisfied with what exists. That does not mean that they are unhappy, but I think that they're not satisfied with what they see and what they learn. This then evokes the desire to create something completely new and innovative.

Creative people seem to have a certain way of thinking that sets them apart from other people. Otherwise we would get same results from everybody. But I also feel that it's quite important to communicate the results of a creative process appropriately in order to make people comprehend that what they're looking at is innovative, different and individual. So it's necessary to involve people and make them understand that, if you want to be really innovative, you must overrule the tendency of making compromises every time you create something just to please everybody.

> ... if you want to be really innovative, you must overrule the tendency of making compromises

Roland Heiler. *Photo: Porsche Design Group*

Something that has always motivated me personally is the fun and the joy that I find in drawing and in using that tool to explore new fields, new shapes and new functions. This definitely has something to do with a lot of restlessness and the constant desire to explore paths that are significantly different from the existing ones. But then, of course, there's always that nagging thought, "If the solution is not perfect, is the idea good enough to pursue it further?"

My early fascination with cars

As a child, I had a couple of interests. I loved illustrating and drawing above all, but beyond that – already from a very early age onward – I've always had a huge interest in cars. When I combined the two, I always ended up drawing cars. I mean, I didn't just copy existing cars but actually drew fictitious cars that didn't exist at all. And this is how I got involved with this particular kind of creative work.

My parents were moderately sympathetic with what I did. They supported me and they were certainly not throwing any stones in my way. But creativity did not assume quite as prominent a position in their lives as it did in mine.

From a genetic point of view, my grandfather is probably the one person

Family of products designed by the Porsche Design Studio. *Photo: Porsche Design Group*

most responsible for my interest in drawing. While he was a soldier in the German army during World War II, he sustained his need to be creative by carving landscapes into army mess kits. These mess kits were metal "dishes" for eating out of that soldiers carried around with them while doing service in the army. He was actually a very, very good artist, but he never got a chance to develop his skills, not even when he returned to normal life after the war ended. But for me, he was my one big influence.

I didn't go through what you would probably consider the conventional way of becoming a designer. After I had finished grammar school, I wanted to work with my hands instead of going to university. Therefore, I started an apprenticeship at the Porsche factory in Stuttgart. During this apprenticeship period, I spent some time in Weissach, Germany, at the Porsche research and development center. At the same time, my father gave me a book entitled *Wheels*. It was then that, for the first time, I saw the profession of a car designer actually described in a book, and I thought, "Wow, this is exactly what I want to do."

This is also how I first became aware of Ferdinand Porsche, his captivation with car design and his creative philosophy in general, which not only fascinated me but also exerted an important influence on me and my future activities.

Another person who became very important to me later on was Richard Soderberg, a graduate of the 1960s and also very much involved in car design. Being chief designer at Porsche at the time, he was an incredibly talented artist who supported me as a mentor.

Another car design-oriented person that I would like to mention in this context is Tony Lapine. He was the person who actually made it possible for me to study design. I met Tony Lapine when he was head of the Porsche styling department, and he let me join him and work in the design studio as an apprentice. After about one year, Tony went to the human relations board member and asked him to give the go-ahead for my studying abroad. So they sent me to the Royal College of Art in London to learn the profession properly. There, I graduated with a Master's Degree.

My career as a designer

Since then, I've been working for car companies for most of my professional life. I spent several years in the United States where I became head designer and, later, managing director of the Porsche Styling Studio in Huntington Beach, California.

Since 2004, I've been responsible for the Porsche Design Studio in Zell am See, Austria. The Porsche Design Studio is a 100 percent subsidiary of the

Porsche Design Group, with its main focus being high-quality, luxury accessories, as well as industrial design.

Most of the time, we create personal luxury products such as watches, eyewear, writing instruments and leather goods. More recently, Porsche Design has expanded its product range to include sports equipment, kitchen design and furniture. In addition, we realize projects such as sailboats, motor yachts and aircraft interiors for industrial clients who are not connected with the Porsche Design brand.

I love the fact that we encompass a very unusual range of creative projects at Porsche Design. Whereas my past experience has been mainly in transportation design, the design team in Zell am See comprises both transportation and product designers, which is why we're able to handle so many different product concepts.

> The biggest satisfaction, after you have created a product and you know how much blood, sweat and tears went into it, is when you finally discover it in the showroom and see how people are enjoying it.

I've tried to keep a good balance between my creative and my administrative activities. Most of my life I've worked creatively, and that's, of course, what I like to do most of all. But lately, my managerial and business responsibilities have increased more and more. However, our design studio is still small enough to enable me to be intimately involved in all product development activities. I talk to my designers every day and discuss ideas with them – so our communication is very good. This is a healthy balance and I enjoy the way it works.

As a manager, what I appreciate most is the opportunity to be involved in the development of so many different products and in the creation of these products. The biggest satisfaction, after you have created a product and you know how much blood, sweat and tears went into it, is when you finally discover it in the showroom and see how people are enjoying it.

It's wonderfully satisfying when you have the impression that people see the product exactly in the way you meant it to look and work.

How we handle creative tasks

Our working procedure is very distinct. Typically, when we get a new assignment from a customer, we start with a brainstorming session that includes me, as well as the entire designer team, and we discuss various possibilities of how to approach the project. It is very important to get as many brains as possible involved in the early stages of product creation.

Later on – during the product development process and in the refinement

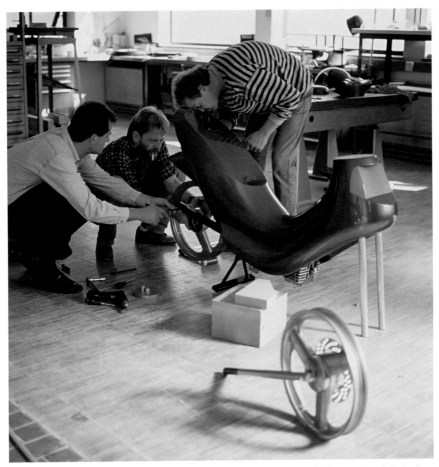

Model shop at the Porsche Design Studio. *Photo: Porsche Design Group*

and finalization stages – you can reduce the number of people involved. But I believe that in the beginning, one brain, even if it's a very creative brain, is not enough, unless you know exactly, right from the start, what kind of style or what kind of solution you want to apply to the product. In that case, of course, you need less input and you can just put the right guy to it. But, in most cases, this is not applicable because the critical issue is to find the most exciting solution.

I've heard that, at some companies, the designer teams have an interesting program by which some of the key people working for them use one day every week by themselves in order to experiment on their own and come up with new ideas.

I think this is actually a great recipe for encouraging creativity in the professional field. At Porsche Design, we practice a variation of that in the second stage of design development, the stage that follows the initial brainstorming session. This is when everybody in the group has the same amount of knowledge and information about the assignment and the designers go back to their desks and start thinking on their own about all the aspects of the problem. Then, later on, we all get together again and we communicate and discuss what the designers have come up with.

Creativity often requires risks

Some of the most exciting and satisfying creative solutions are those that turn up unexpectedly. In view of the huge landscape of products that exist around the world today, this is often very helpful because it can lead to unique solutions.

There are many examples from both the past and the present of companies that have taken the risk of introducing a new, unique concept for a product. Sometimes such products are definitely the most passionately loved ones, but they can also be the most debated ones in a company.

New, unique concepts almost always excite a lot of discussion and often get outright resistance. Businesspeople, more often than not, are conservative and don't want to take any risks. They would rather focus on products that, they feel, will please everybody.

Sometimes a market survey determines whether or not consumers will be comfortable with a new concept. Decisions then have to be made whether to proceed with a new creative concept, whether to abandon it, or whether – and to what an extent – compromises should be made before introducing the product into the market.

This is one of the many issues that every industrial designer has to face occasionally. We get some pretty cynical comments from salespeople whose attitude often is, "I don't care whether the product has a unique design, I just need a product that sells."

> Some of the most exciting and satisfying creative solutions are those that turn up unexpectedly.

Sometimes, there's quite a lot of tension between the design and the sales mindsets. There are times, of course, when designers take things a little too far to the intellectual level in the product-creation process. While this is part of what they are expected to do, they must also take commercial aspects into account and that the consumer's point of view may not necessarily be on the same intellectual level as the designer's vision.

There are different ways of looking at this.

Design managers, of course, have to be very aware of the paramount importance for companies and brands to position themselves properly in order to support a product and make it a commercial success. And, as the design manager of Porsche Design, I fully subscribe to this principle.

On the other hand, even if a product is not a big success on the market, its unique design may get front-page attention in publications and thus contribute to the company's overall image in the consumer's mind. So, both aspects are very important and need a good balance.

At the end of the day, of course, designers are people who work for the company that is trying to sell its products. And so, to please the consumer, designers must create products that are both handsomely designed and function well. In other words, the solutions must please the hand as well as the eye. And that's probably the hardest thing to accomplish – to create products that fulfill both of those requirements.

The Porsche Design philosophy

Professor Ferdinand Alexander Porsche, designer of the Porsche 911 and grandson of the Porsche founder, opened the Porsche Design Studio in Stuttgart in 1972, which was moved to Zell am See two years later.

The Porsche 911 quickly became the quintessential sports car and a design classic, along with many other products that Professor Porsche designed.

Over the following decades, he and a dozen employees created classic men's accessories such as watches, glasses and writing utensils that were marketed worldwide under the "Porsche Design" brand. At the same time, he developed many industrial products and household and consumer goods for internationally recognized clients – including streetcars for the city of Vienna – under the "Design by F.A. Porsche" brand.

To support the Porsche reputation for excellence, one of the key issues for us at Porsche Design is that our products must reflect a very clear position that defines the Porsche Design world. I'm referring here to Porsche Design products, not the Porsche cars, even though the philosophy that guides the technical and visual solutions is very similar for both.

So the products designed by the Porsche Design group always need to meet certain requirements that will make their design approach timeless. Porsche Design products are technically inspired, of the highest quality and made from the finest material. Their design must therefore be true to their inner structure. Their function is just as important as their look – no more design than necessary!

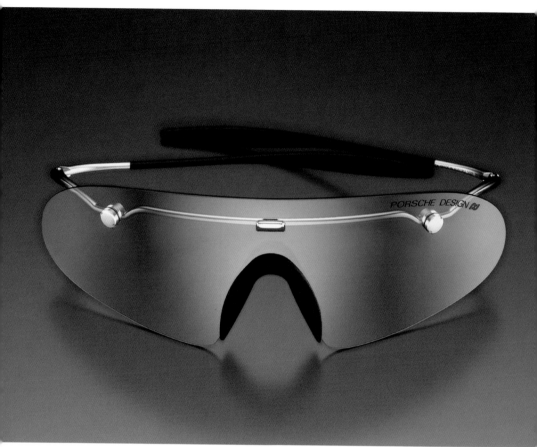

Porsche Design Sport Sunglasses. *Photo: Porsche Design Group*

The Porsche Design F09 sunglasses are a good example that I'd like to use to illustrate our design approach.

We've been focusing on sunglasses ever since the early days of Porsche Design. When wraparound sunglasses became popular, we designed wraparound glasses that embodied the Porsche Design philosophy. They wrapped comfortably around the contours of your face, and they looked beautiful.

However, we soon became aware of one big problem: when you wanted to put the glasses in your pocket, they were rather bulky and difficult to tuck away because of their curvature.

So our team sat down and said, "What if we created a pair of sunglasses that make a wraparound statement when you wear them, but fold very flat when you want to put them in your pocket?"

After exploring various approaches to achieving this, one of our creative guys came up with a concept that was particularly interesting. This designer works slightly different from the others in the group: he hardly ever draws anything but makes three-dimensional cardboard models, which make his concepts easy to comprehend. That way, he was able to demonstrate the folding and unfolding movement of the glasses in 3-D. It was a very generic model, but it explained the fundamentals in such a way that they were easy to understand.

The solution was a unique design concept that allows you to fold the glasses completely flat to a height of 9 mm when you want to put them in your pocket. Then, when you want to wear them, you can unfold them and the frame actually "forces" the polycarbonate lens to take the form of a wraparound contour.

> I believe that it's of primary importance to have a design signature that communicates a clear identity.

One model has been on the market for some time now. The next generation, a model taken one step further from the original, will be launched soon. With that model, you don't even have to do anything but open the hinges, and the polycarbonate screen will then automatically move into position. So we've basically taken a new concept, perfected it and brought it to a new level.

I think the R09 sunglasses are a good example of how we function at Porsche Design and how we handle the design process: always creating a unique product that functions well and looks beautiful.

Our philosophy clearly derives from the Bauhaus doctrine, which was an important movement in Germany in the early days of the development of industrial design. It stood for design simplicity and good product engineering. I would describe the Porsche Design philosophy as a European-influenced design language or, more precisely, a German-influenced design language.

Most importantly, I believe that it's of primary importance to have a design signature that communicates a clear identity. While it may not appeal to everybody, it will certainly attract people who love and seek this type of contemporary product design and ideology.

My own philosophy about creativity

I think there are many great philosophical and psychological differences among creative people and throughout the creative field.

If you look at fine artists, you may find some of them who are willing to live just on the basis of personal satisfaction, and who are happy with the results of their own creative work.

Other people involved with creative endeavors, such as writers and music-

Selection of products designed by Porsche Design Studio. *Photo: Porsche Design Group*

ians, as well as people in other creative disciplines, may feel that recognition by the general public of what they create is a major concern to them. These people want to feel that they're contributing something to the community, and, in a way, that's what they are actually doing.

Still other creative people who may be incredibly innovative are also incredibly good marketing people. These people crave for feedback from the media. Others, who may be equally creative, prefer to work at their desks and feel happy when they're not bothered by anyone.

So, there are many different personalities in the creative environment.

As for myself, I've always been a team player. I'm not one of those designers who like to point to a product and say, "Hey, look what I've created." I'm very proud of having been involved in the creation of many products during my time with the car company as well as during my association with Porsche Design.

When I don't work, I spend most of the time with my family. I also love to drive in my vintage 1963 Porsche. And since my wife also likes driving around in the old car, we take part in all kinds of vintage car rallies. This is our hobby – something we love to do.

Professionally, I like to believe that I've succeeded in influencing some people's lives in a positive way by helping to create products that transmit a degree of honesty and emotion and also function in a way that appeals to people who love good design.

All this may not seem to be the most important concern in a world that is struggling with so many serious problems. But I believe that when you create a product that gives others pleasure, you contribute, no matter how infinitesimally, to the joys of life.

MILTON GLASER

Being a design generalist

Milton Glaser, one of most admired graphic and architectural designers in the world, is both a practitioner and an enthusiastic teacher of graphic arts. Well known for his posters and prints, his numerous accomplishments include the co-founding of Push Pin Studio in 1954 and of New York Magazine *in 1968, as well as decorative design programs for New York restaurants. He has enjoyed one-man shows at the Centre Georges Pompidou in Paris and the Museum of Modern Art in New York. His numerous awards include the 2004 Lifetime Achievement Award from the Smithsonian Cooper-Hewitt, National Design Museum for his long-time contribution to the contemporary practice of design.*

Everybody wants to be creative. One of the nice things about being "creative" is you that you can claim it without being able to measure it. It's a generic term that is frequently used but is not very carefully defined. It also exists as a noun, "the creatives," which is an abomination. Imagine calling people "the creatives." Clearly, creativity is too complex to be reduced to catch a simple idea.

It's hard to tell what really motivates creative people. No one really knows what drives them. Someone wise once said the mind is a poor instrument to examine the self.

You can recognize people that move in the world and seem to be creative and like to make things – but explaining *why* they do it is a fruitless task. There is no analysis that is going to be a definitive one, or one that would apply to all creative individuals.

So, what *is* creativity?

When you talk about being creative, you have to distinguish between people who truly invent and make things that have not existed before, or clever people who adapt other people's ideas.

Ad agencies and art studios are full of non-creative people who describe themselves as creative. One can be very clever by knowing what to steal from others. That is not my definition of creativity.

Milton Glaser. *Photo: Matthew Klein*

To be truly creative, you have to invent a vocabulary or perception that has almost no precedent. This is very difficult to accomplish. Most of us live off other people's ideas.

In advertising and design, one must stay within the existing understanding of the audience, because work that is produced and not understood produces hostility and confusion.

So the first boundary you have to deal with is, "What does your audience already understand?" Something new is, by that definition, incomprehensible. So what you always have to deal with in communication is how much "new" will be acceptable to your audience?

New ideas have constraints

If you have a new idea, very often it has to be wrapped in what is already known. That's a significant constraint. And that's why most of the work that is done in an agency or a design office is, generally speaking, not new and is basically a variant of some idea that already has resonance or understanding in the culture.

It's not much of a surprise that people are easily startled into rejection. The balance between old and new, I might say, is the critical balance of advertising and communication. When people talk about a new idea, you must ask, "Is it new or simply an old idea resurfaced a little bit?"

The creative impulse is intrinsic to our species. We are a form-making species. One could claim that form making, intrinsically, is creative. On a species level, creativity is necessary because that's the way we humans adapt to our circumstances and why we have become so successful as a species.

Fundamentally, creativity is a survival mechanism. The reason why our species has survived is our brain structure. It made us more adaptive and responsive to the context that we're living in. So we might say that creativity is basically a way of surviving.

> Fundamentally, creativity is a survival mechanism.

We all must find a way to survive. Some people have to survive by *suppressing* their creativity. A lot of people in ordinary work situations have to basically be less creative than they really are in order to adapt to their existing condition of their environment. You can't be more creative in your professional life than the environment is willing to accept.

Professionalism vs. creativity

Early in my life, my aspiration was to become a professional because professionals seemed to know everything – not to mention that they got paid for doing their work.

I Love NY logo. *Courtesy of Milton Glaser Inc.*

Later, after working for a while, I discovered that that professionalism was itself a limitation that can discourage creativity. Keep in mind that the nature of professional life is to minimize risk. Minimizing risk is what you must do.

If you want to get your car repaired, you don't want the repair guy to be "creative" and invent a new way to repair your transmission. You want him to do it the way he's always done it.

Or, if you need brain surgery, you wouldn't want the doctor to experiment to find a new way to connect your nerve endings. You hope he will do it the way it has worked in the past.

Professionalism discourages transgression because transgression encompasses the possibility of failure and if you want to be a professional, your instinct is to not to fail. It is to repeat success.

So, you can see that, intrinsically, there's a conflict between professionalism that calls for *minimizing* risk, while creativity *encourages* risk. Reconciling these contradictions is not easy.

> ... there's a conflict between professionalism that calls for *minimizing* risk, while creativity *encourages* risk.

So, where do new ideas come from?

In absolute terms, what we call creative usually has no precedent. Truly creative people, like Picasso, did work throughout his life on ideas not entirely understandable. Ultimately, Picasso's work changed the paradigm.

I'm convinced that there are so many ideas in the universe, that as soon as I hear or see something, I have more ideas than I know how to deal with.

Where don't ideas come from is the real question.

I do some exercises with students, which depend on mind reading and the realization that we don't know what we know.

You look at a book on Coptic painting and you'll have a hundred ideas about how to interpret and use it for some other purpose. Ideas come from everywhere.

Personally, my greatest source of ideas comes from reading about other things – anthropology, behavior, or brain structure. Where they *don't* come from – where they've never come from – is from what other people, my contemporaries, are doing at the time. Everything that is being done is already over.

Ideas seem to come from our own personal histories, those of other generations, and the visual history of the world.

I've always had the sense there is a continuity of ideas in human history that we depend on. Ideas come from this universal reservoir we have of our own past and those of other generations, and also the visual history of the world. The arts and crafts movement alone, for instance, can be a source of thousands of ideas. The Viennese Succession – thousands of ideas. The Renaissance – thousands of ideas. To repeat the issue – it may be that there are too many ideas.

About my career

I'm a designer and have been practicing for a very long time.

I decided to be an artist at the age of five. It was a miracle. My cousin, who was fifteen at the time, came to the house to baby-sit for me. He had a paper bag and, to entertain me, he said, "Would you like to see a bird?" I thought he had a bird in the bag. I said, "Yes," and he pulled a pencil out of the bag and drew a bird on the side of the bag. It was the first time I had actually seen someone draw something that looked like the object depicted.

I was absolutely astonished. I thought it was the most remarkable thing I'd ever seen. And at that moment, I decided that this was what I was going to spend my life doing. If I had to isolate a single event, that was probably the moment that made me aware that making things is what I wanted to spend my life doing.

The decision to be an artist was very mysterious because, at the age of five, you have no idea of what it means to be an artist. Nevertheless, something had happened to me. Partially, it was the sense of the miraculous when my cousin drew that bird. Seeing the transformation of an idea into an image was something so powerful that I was incapable of resisting it.

I had one resistant parent and one encouraging parent, which I think is a very good combination. My mother made me believe that I could do anything. My father said, "Show me." It's a very good combination, because the father represents the resistance of the world that you're going to face, sooner or later. But the birthright that you get from an encouraging mother is that you believe you can do anything, which stays with you for life. My mother gave me the sense of self-assurance. My father's resistance made me develop perseverance.

I was fortunate to live in New York City because the opportunity for education in New York City was, at that time, unparalleled anywhere. I started a class in life drawing when I was twelve. I went to The High School of Music and Art where the emphasis was on both academic studies and artistic ones.

Then, after attending and graduating from Cooper Union and getting a Fulbright scholarship, I went to Bologna, Italy, where I spent a significant amount of time, learning how to draw all over again.

After a couple of years there, I came back to the United States, and in 1954 started Push Pin Studio with Ed Sorel and Seymour Chwast. Seymour and I ran Push Pin Studio for twenty years.

> The great thing about design is that you never really stop learning.

I love to work. There is nothing more interesting to me. I feel very fortunate being able to work in a category where I still have a lot to learn. The great thing about design is that you never really stop learning.

That is a great benefit, as opposed to the usual path of professional life, where you attain a certain level of success and then cruise on your accomplishment. With design, you can maintain your interest, your enthusiasm and your sense of astonishment until the day you die.

I have no real hobby. I have done little besides teaching and working. The great fear in my life is not having a day's work to do.

I read a little every evening and I read a lot on the weekends. This is a benefit of not having any hobbies. The idea of going out to play golf every Sunday morning is a complete horror to me. I don't go to movies and I don't go to the theater. I am an ignorant man.

There is nothing that satisfies me as much as working, and reading, and thinking about the nature of design and culture. I deeply want to die at my desk. Work is my life.

What might be considered a hobby is collecting art. Shirley, my wife, and I collect art that provides inspiration to me. We have a collection of nineteenth-century lithographs, Persian miniatures, and a large collection of African sculpture.

I have a special interest in African sculpture. To me, African sculpture is one of the greatest examples of human accomplishment. These people have no education really in the sense that you and I had education, but they create. They grow up learning how to live under dire circumstances. And this is instructive because it shows that people without our education can be enormously compelling and imaginative.

When people ask me what I do, I say that I am a designer. All the while, I like to keep it ambiguous. I like the idea that people don't know exactly what I do.

I like to consider myself a generalist in the field of design. I like the idea of doing different things – interiors, sculpture, lighting, graphics, posters and drawings.

> I'm very interested in the idea that there is a social role for designers

I like that because I think that's a way of basically moving toward what you don't know so that you don't plateau and keep repeating what you do know. Staying open-minded has been essentially my device for avoiding boredom. And indifference.

I love teaching. I've been teaching forever. My universal code for any design activity in any subject is:

(1)   Identify your audience
(2)   Clarify your message – what is it you want to tell them to do?
(3)   Decide on how that message can be most effectively shaped in terms of style, technique and medium.

This process can apply to anything you're ever going to design. But only in step three do you get to such issues as style and beauty. These are the kinds of questions that most people think design is about. But what I like to examine is the steps that precede those final decisions. The most important step of all is the nature of the audience.

In that way, I have done a variety of things. I have worked on a number of restaurants, such as the Trattoria Dell'Arte in New York. I designed that entire restaurant – interiors, menus, signage and the design of china. With Joe Baum, the great restaurateur, I worked on the Rainbow Room, and Windows on the World.

I've also been involved in several universities and museum projects. An example is Stony Brook University in New York, a project that has lasted ten years and involved all aspects of campus life: communication, interiors, signage, advertising, products, and publications.

More recently, I have been working with the Minneapolis Art Institute. We modified their name slightly to Minneapolis Institute of Art in order to create the word "MIA". And we suggested that they could achieve a unique image by reaching into their collection to establish the continuity of visual history, such as going from a Monet to contemporary photography, or from Chinese robes to a Gustav Klimt. Or from Elvis Presley to a Roman sculpture.

Another interesting project was the Rubin Museum. It was the conversion of the famous old Barney's clothing store on 17th Street and Seventh Avenue in New York City into a museum that features Himalayan art. We did a 17-foot gilded copper wall and established the tone of the entry and the spirit and look visual communications.

I'm very interested in the idea that there is a social role for designers, and that this is a moment in history when that role has to be practiced. The principle of design citizenship is very important to me. I think that it's imperative for designers to think more about their effect on the world.

Darfur poster. *Courtesy of Milton Glaser Inc.*

My personal response to today's conditions here and around the world has led me to become more active in civic life. As designers, we have been concerned about our role in society for a very long time. It's important to remember that even modernism had social reform as its basic principle, but the need to act seems more imperative than ever.

That said, I believe that design's effect on society has to be part of what art and design schools teach.

I teach at the School of Visual Arts and got them involved in a follow-up to the events of 9/11. Some time ago, I did the poster "I ❤ New York," which, I believe, most New Yorkers, and even people elsewhere, are familiar with.

After 9/11, I produced a follow-up poster "I ❤ New York more than ever" that was distributed around the city by students of the School of Visual Arts, as well as being wrapped around a million copies of the *Daily News*. For another poster expressing empathy for the plight of Africa, I went to the School of Visual Arts and asked if they would cooperate in distributing it, and they spent $75,000 in buying bus kiosk advertising. The bus kiosk people threw in another 175 locations, because they were sympathetic.

Of course, in the case of personal intervention, the design problem is how to become visible and how to enter into the bloodstream of the culture.

In summary – staying creative involves discarding your past accomplishments or at least building on them.

What you don't want to do is get stuck on any series of ideas. I never feel that my ideas are not susceptible to revision, even though I've invested a lot of time in them. We tend to feel invested in things we spend time on, like a bank account that needs to be protected.

My feeling is, you can invest a lot of time on an idea – but if, at any time, you feel that it's used up – bail out. I'm a great believer in keeping works organic and not thinking of the time you've invested, like this "money in the bank" thing. I try to kick over anything midway in the process, or even after I've completed it, if I recognize that it's not doing what I want it to do, or if it simply repeats what I already know.

So, I've done a lot of things. I love the fact that I have been able to do these things and I love best that I have been able to define a career as a design generalist, which has always been my predominant interest.

My hope is that my work has been able to influence future design generations. Other people will have to evaluate whether and how this has helped to enhance the way we live.

The "green" room at the Trattoria Dell'Arte restaurant in New York designed
by Milton Glaser. *Courtesy of Milton Glaser Inc.*

The "Italian" sushi bar at the Trattoria Dell'Arte restaurant in New York, designed by Milton Glaser.
Courtesy of Milton Glaser Inc.

CHUCK CLOSE

Decoding the mysterious process of art

Chuck Close, the American photorealistic painter, is known for his large portraits based on his unique grid work. The creative process he uses to achieve his art is as important to him as the finished product. He is also a master printmaker who has over the course of more than thirty years pushed the boundaries of traditional printmaking in remarkable ways. His work was first exhibited at the New York Museum of Modern Art in 1973. His paintings now hang in the world's most prestigious museums and he is celebrated as one of the most influential figurative painters of our time.

One thing that makes creativity in my field different from other activities is the desire to not go with the conventional wisdom.

Conventional wisdom is almost always mediocre, because most people agree that a problem should be solved the same way. I think that artists try to put themselves into their own idiosyncratic personal corner where nobody else's answers will fit.

In our society, problem *solving* is greatly overappreciated. Problem *creation* is, in fact, much more interesting. Because, if you ask yourself a really interesting question and no one else's answers will fit, that will kick open a door that you can go through and follow your own path to wherever it goes. One way to distinguish yourself from the pack is to try and follow your own path with art, so that somebody standing in front of your work will not be thinking about another artist.

> I think the most exciting thing in the visual arts is to see something that actually does not look like art.

Lately, for a lot of younger artists, appropriation is the prime modus operandi, and that's antithetical to the way I came up. It's like sampling in popular music. You take something that already exists and you put your personal stamp on it. But it's going to look like someone else's art or it will not look like art.

I think the most exciting thing in the visual arts is to see something that actually does not look like art. So what do you do?

Chuck Close. *Courtesy of Pace Wildenstein, New York. Photo: Laura Miller*

Chuck Close in New York studio 2006. *Photo: Richard Gerstman*

How I learned about art

I always wanted to be an artist from five years on. I studied art at the age of eight. And when I was eleven, I was drawing from nude models. When I saw my first Jackson Pollock at age eleven in an art museum in Seattle, I was outraged. "This doesn't look like art. This can't possibly be art." But within a matter of a few days, I was dripping paint all over my figurative paintings.

Similarly, when I first saw Andy Warhol's soup cans and the Brillo boxes stacked up in an art gallery, it looked to me like a supermarket, not like an art gallery. And Frank Stella's black stripe paintings didn't seem to have anything that looked like art either.

At any given time, the resultant outside shape of the art world is a sort of amoeba shape – a wing sticks out this way, and a wing sticks out that way. Then someone comes along and operates outside that shape and, since it doesn't look like art or feel like art, it often outrages people.

But pretty soon, the art world goes out and envelopes that isolated island that's out of the mainstream and tugs it into the mother ship of art. And now that the art world has incorporated it, it's now also art. The resultant shape of the art world is different now because that artist was there.

So this is what I think we chase. We chase the experience of looking at other people's art, and we chase it in our own careers and our own lives, trying not to demonstrate just that we know what art looks like, but trying to find a way to keep moving.

When you no longer want to do something, you simply construct a set of limitations that will prevent you from doing that anymore, and then you do something else. For me this is an interesting process, because I've had to keep all the balls in the air for thirty or forty years. You have to keep changing, you have to keep delivering surprises, and you have to keep yourself engaged.

If I'm talking to you and I'm boring you because I've said the same thing over and over, you start giving me body language like, "It must be time to leave." Visual art is a form of communication, and if the reaction from your audience to your work is that it no longer has any urgency or any sense of freshness – if they feel that you've plowed that field way too many times – the audience will let you know.

You may also just tire of the repetition yourself and want to change the experience you have in the studio. Every time you change your experience, it will change the product that you create, and the audience will react to it differently. And that is how you keep moving.

This is antithetical to success in many other fields, where once you have hit upon something that has gotten traction, or people feel is successful, there is tremendous pressure on you to just keep on producing that product. That's not the way it works in the art world.

How I became an artist

If I lived on a desert island with no one around, I seriously wonder whether I would make art. I'd be going crazy if I was carrying on a conversation with somebody who was not there. And I really believe in the communicative power of the visual arts and that it's made to be shared.

And I felt this as a young child when I was profoundly learning disabled. I was a bad student, and I was not athletic. But the one thing I could do was to make art. I did puppet shows and magic acts, all of which were to entertain the troops and keep the kids around me.

In the 1940s and 1950s, nobody knew about dyslexia or learning disabilities. You were simply dumb and lazy – a shirker, a malingerer. My report card said, "Charles's mind wanders and he looks out the window." I could never add or subtract and I still don't know the multiplication tables. I use the spots on dominos to add and subtract. For six and five – it is six, seven, eight, nine, ten, eleven – using the dominos.

So art saved my life in school, because this is how I showed my teachers that I was interested in the material and in the course, even when I was unable to spit back names and dates in an exam. I would make a 20-foot long mural of the Lewis and Clark trail and drag it in for extra credit. That mitigated my poor test performance in the classroom.

> I was looking for something … and art was the one thing that made me feel special.

My mother was a classical pianist who had hoped to have a concert career. But the Depression pretty much did away with that dream and she taught piano in the home most of my life. I actually was a musician as well. My father was an inventor, a jack-of-all-trades, and a sheet metalworker for the Army Air Corps.

We were a family that valued creativity. But we lived in Everett, Washington, at that time a poor white trash mill town, where nobody aspired to do anything other than to work in the mill. Even today, virtually my entire class still lives in the same town and works in the same mill that their mothers and fathers did.

I don't know how I escaped. I was looking for something – everyone needs to feel special – and art was the one thing that made me feel special. It was the one thing I could do that my friends could not. I don't think I was any more gifted and talented than anyone else in our town, but I was hungrier and I wanted more. I had no other talents and I wasn't any good at anything other than art. So I put all my eggs in that basket.

Most people are good at too many things, and then they can't figure out what they want to do. In our society, when somebody says that a person is focused, they really mean that the person is very narrow. And I think I was very narrow. I was going headlong to pursue one thing. I was on this highway, and I didn't want an off ramp. I distinguished myself from my colleagues by trying harder, by being more committed and working harder.

Since I had not taken any algebra, geometry, physics or chemistry in high school, I could not have gotten into any college in the country, but I was a product of the state of Washington's open enrollment policy. Junior colleges took every taxpayer's son or daughter, no matter what, and you could make up for a year of deficiencies once you were there.

I began to do research into what was required in each of the classes. Since I couldn't spell anything, I took classes where I could dictate a paper and have someone else type it. All of a sudden, I was doing very well in school.

This was a junior college. After two years there, I transferred to the University of Washington and I did extremely well there. When I graduated, I was totally surprised to find that I had the highest grade point average of anyone in the art school. This was because I had worked so hard to find an area in which I could excel.

I became the University of Washington's compromise candidate to the Yale summer school, which is the out of town tryouts for Yale. At that time, I actually had no desire to go there. I wanted to stay in the state of Washington just to paint.

But when I graduated with my B.A. from the University of Washington in 1961, I was eligible for the draft. And since the people who knew me at Yale summer school liked me, they moved me to the top of the waiting list for Yale and I was enrolled.

Yale changed my life. It was the most incredible experience of my life. The graduate school at Yale had a phenomenal program. At that particular time, my classmates were Richard Serra, Nancy Graves, Brice Marden, Bob and Sylvia Mangold, and Jennifer Bartlett. It's like a who's who of art of our generation.

I had a Fulbright scholarship to Vienna. In fact, we had seven Fulbright's within the art school. So we all went to Europe together and often visited each other. After returning to the United States, I taught for two years in Massachusetts before coming to New York. There we all helped each other, and it was a great time to be a young artist in New York.

How my art changed

About forty years ago I was making big, broad, flat, messy abstractions. They were very tentative. I would put paint on, and scrape it off, and put it on, and scrape it off and never knew when I was finished. They looked a lot like de Kooning.

I had gone through school getting all kinds of scholarships and pats on the head for demonstrating that I knew how to make art. But when, after graduating, I found myself in my own studio, I thought, "Where am I in this room? I

mean, de Kooning is in this room, and other people are in this room, but where am I in this room?"

That's when I decided to change every aspect of my work. Since I depended so much on color, I decided to work only in black and white. Since my hand made art marks and art shapes, I decided to work from photographs so the shapes would have to be the shapes in the photograph and not some art shape. And I made the decision to use only black paint on white canvas because I wanted every mark to still be there when I was done. That forced me to commit early, and not count on being able to change things later.

To enlarge a small photograph onto a big canvas, I decided to use a grid system. The grid has been around since ancient Egypt, and from the Renaissance on, it was a standard scaling-up device. So, even though all my paintings appeared to be continuous tone, they were in fact made incrementally in building blocks as a grid.

> Sometimes the work that you hate teaches you more than the work that you love.

Over the years, the incremental units have been fingerprints, wads of pulp paper, scribbles, anything that I could think of that made an individual incremental building block.

In the paintings that I'm making now, what used to be one-sixth of an inch square is now three-and-a-half inches. This gives me a lot of room in which to put a lot of stuff. I wanted to literally not have any difference in touch or in attitude for those areas that make a symbolic area, like an eye, or a piece of background. And that's pretty much how my work has evolved.

What influenced me

People may think that the kind of work we do requires inspiration. I have always felt that inspiration is for amateurs. If you wait for inspiration, you will never get anything done. I don't know any serious, important contemporary artist who would wait around to be inspired. It's the dumbest concept that you can think of.

We are the conglomerates of all our experiences. Sometimes the work that you hate teaches you more than the work that you love. Sometimes the work that annoys you will get under your skin and change your mind about what art should be.

The people who have been the biggest influence on me have contaminated my work, have contaminated my life and they have been hard to purge. When you love something, you want to incorporate it into your work. But then it's not your work – it's that other person's work. And it's very hard to purge it, because you're throwing away things you love so much.

At this point in my life, I realize that I am putting a lot of de Kooning color into my paintings, but I'm doing it in such a way that it doesn't look like de Kooning. So you absorb things that become part of your nature and part of you, but you have to find a way to refashion them, and forge them into a tool for your own specific use, rather than using the other person's tool.

My creative process

My paintings, although they appear to be mathematical, are "found and felt." My father-in-law is an engineer, and he used to make fun of me because of the way that I gridded these things off and I didn't use a calculator or anything. Especially for the diagonal grid ones, it's hard to figure out how many squares are going to fit onto a canvas and exactly what size they are going to be.

So I would take a piece of paper of a certain length and slide it along the edge of the painting to see how many squares I could get. If I would get too few, I would fold it smaller and slide that along until it came out right. It's different to "find it" than it is to superimpose a mathematical grid system on top of it. But I have always found ways to work in which I am sneaking up on what I want, rather than conceptualizing it.

Let me give you an example of the thought process. First, there is under-painting, which is sort of a stream of consciousness, almost as if you're writing the first draft of a novel. What I'm doing in the underpainting process is simply putting different colors down. If the same colors were underneath, the correcting colors that I put on top would also be pretty much the same. But if I start with a yellow, then a pink, then a blue, then a purple–orange and then a purple, the correcting colors that go on top have got to be different.

This process was partially to overcome the problem of the palette. I believe that when you make decisions on a palette, you are making decisions out of context. You hope that these are the correct decisions when you drop them into the context of the painting, or into the rectangles. I wanted to find everything in the rectangle and make all the decisions in context, adjacent to squares that are already finished and in anticipation of squares that I've yet to make.

Here's an analogy. Using the palette is the equivalent of shooting an arrow

Right: Self Portrait 2004–2005 (work in progress) © Chuck Close. Courtesy of Pace Wildenstein, New York. Photographs: Laura Miller

directly at a bulls-eye. You hope that you made the color decision that will be exactly what you want.

My method is more like golf, which is the only sport where you move from general to specific in an ideal number of discrete, correcting moves. The first stroke is just out there, the second stroke corrects that, and the third corrects that further. By then, hopefully, you're on the green, and in four or five strokes you have placed the ball in this very specific three-inch diameter circle that you could not even see from where you teed off. You found it while you moved through the landscape making various course corrections. So that's the process that I use to make my paintings.

As I move along, I may do something that is wrong before it is right. Then I say to myself, "Well, what do I need to do to move it closer to what I want?" So on top of the blue I may put orange. Now, on top of that, what do I need? Well, it's still looking a little too cool, so I put a yellow in the middle of that. Or, if I've gone too far that way, I drop a cool color – a green or something – back in the middle of that. This is a very different thought process than conceptualizing something and then just executing it.

It's issues like this that I build my work around. Embedded in the work itself are indications of the process. You can see what colors are underneath and you can see what colors are on top. And I drop crumbs along the trail, Hansel and Gretel style, for people to pick up if they want to engage themselves with the process. If, however, they don't want to do that, or if they want the imagery just to wash over them as an experience, they can do that without having to analyze the methodology at all.

This is not unlike music. A musician who listens to a symphony will pick out a particular instrument and realize how it is working to counter another instrument at that particular moment, and may dissect, analyze and maybe not even hear it as a whole the way a layperson would.

I think this happens with artists too. When a painter looks at one of my paintings, it's like a magician watching another magician perform. Would a magician in the audience see the illusion that the magician pulls a rabbit out of a hat, or would he see the device that created the illusion? The answer is: probably a little of both. The magician in the audience would probably see the illusion and also understand how it happened, because of the shared experience of having produced illusions. In the same way, painters know how art happens. They look at a painting and they can figure out the system and the thought process.

Right: Chuck Close. *Self Portrait* 2004–2005. Oil on canvas. 102" x 84" (259.1 x 213.4 cm). *Photo: Ryan McFate*

When I had lunch with my friend Paul Simon the other day, we talked about the creative process. I was struck by the similarity of the refining process of an idea. You do something and you like certain aspects of it. But you don't like some other aspects of it, so you try to get rid of the aspects you do not like, and capitalize on the ones you do like.

> You can have the physicality of art and its qualities speak to you across generations.

He was telling me that his music no longer starts with a melody or words. First comes beat, melody comes second and words always come last. He starts tapping and if he wants a different rhythm, he may change the beat from simple 2/4 beat into something else. Then he may start with some percussion, and begin to put in some words. If he doesn't like those words, he throws those words out and puts in some other words. And slowly the music and the beat evolve.

All this is very similar to what I do – I put some color down, do something to it, and if I don't like those colors, I put in some other colors so my paintings gradually evolve to what I want.

The magical thing about art

When I was a young kid, magazines like *Saturday Evening Post*, *Colliers* and *Look* came to our house. I had a magnifying glass on the coffee table and would scan the art in these magazines and try and figure out the art-making method that the illustrator had used. Although I had never seen a real work of art, I would try to find the brush strokes in the magazine to understand how it happened.

So throughout my life I've been trying to decode this mysterious process – this magical process where paint transcends its physical reality and becomes an illusion, becoming space where there is no space, and things like that.

When I was living in Italy, a few years ago, I loved the humble Roman floor mosaics that you see from Rome all the way down into Tunisia. When you look down at the floor, you see the stones arranged on the flat floor. And just when you're looking at a flat pattern, it begins to work into a lion's head. Then, when you really look at the lion and see the illusion, it flattens back out and becomes a flat floor again. It's that tension between the artificial and the real – the insistent flatness of the surface and the conjured up illusion that makes for a very physical experience for the viewer.

It's also a record of the decisions that that artist made hundreds of years ago. This made it a contemporary experience for me, as if I were looking over the ancient artist's shoulder and seeing him chip the corner of this stone, and slide it into this space. It gave a sense of urgency, as if it were happening right now.

That's really what I think is creativity for the visual arts and where the pleasure lies.

You can have the physicality of art and its qualities speak to you across generations. You see it unfiltered and untranslated, as decisions being made in front of your eyes. And that's one of the magical things about art.

My signs of success

I don't want to own art because owning art is a burden. Thank God, other people are acquisitive or I'd be broke. But I've always worked very hard to get the art into public collections where people who have no financial means can enjoy it. Through the generosity of wealthy philanthropic people, virtually all my art is in public collections, which I'm very happy about.

I don't know whether my paintings have influenced the way people look at art. Probably, nobody is crazy enough to try to make what I make.

It's like with de Kooning and Pollock. De Kooning was attitudinal, out of Cubism and whatever, and that seemed very useful to a lot of artists. Many artists imitated de Kooning. When I first met de Kooning, I said to him, "It's very nice to meet somebody who has made a few more de Koonings than I have made." Many artists learned how to paint making their own de Koonings!

> I think that certain people bend the course of art, or they deflect it, because it's like putting something into a stream and it deflects the course of that stream.

But to me, Pollock was the most influential on art today. He bent the course of our history with his way of working. No one else could truly use his signature style and process. He owned it.

I think that certain people bend the course of art, or they deflect it, because it's like putting something into a stream and it deflects the course of that stream. It will always be different because it interrupted the normal flow.

There are external markers that we have to measure success. My first goal was to have a show in New York before I was thirty. I think I had it a month before I was thirty. I wanted to have a retrospective by the time I was forty, and I was thirty-nine when I got my first retrospective. I wanted a book and now I have many books. I wanted a catalog and by now there are many catalogs. I wanted to be in permanent collections in museums and I'm in almost every one of the larger, contemporary museums in the world. So I've achieved all those outward goals of success.

Appreciating the world of art

But you can't get too complacent with these external markers of success and you can't rest on your laurels. It is a fickle art world out there. The much-despised Impressionists are now the most sought after and the most appreciated. On the other hand, we don't even know some of the most important artists from the turn of the century.

> A work of art is like a vessel or a magic wand and each person can get a different substance out of that vessel.

There are not many fields in which you can go to the grave as an absolute failure in every sense of the word – no critical attention, no sales, no anything – and feel like, "Well, they just didn't understand me. Someday they will all appreciate what I did."

This has sustained countless numbers of artists who never had any trappings of success. If you don't understand the cyclical nature of the art world, you are doomed to a lifetime of alternating pain and happiness, because the art world wants something, then they don't want it – then they might want it again. Only if you understand the cyclical nature of the art world will your relationship with it be a happier one.

One of the characteristics of artists is that you never see an artist retire. That doesn't mean that an artist hasn't made enough money to retire, because I've enough money to retire right now. I could go down to Florida and kick back and drink margaritas the rest of my life and not ever work again. But the days that I don't work move at a glacial speed and are incredibly boring. And the days that I work fly by and I'm extremely happy and fulfilled.

I hope that I've gained more admirers than detractors, but I realize that not everybody likes my work. The day I would get a good review from Hilton Kramer, I'd put my head in the oven. For my first show, he called me a lunatic and said, "It's the trash that washed ashore when the tide of pop art went out." Saying what a lousy artist I was ended up being most of a page of the *New York Times*. I wore his reviews as a badge of honor. I don't really care what reaction one has – I just want a reaction.

Reaction is what I've been getting a great deal more since I've been in a wheelchair. I used to be six foot three and people didn't approach me very much. But being in a wheelchair has cut me down to four foot something and this seems to have made me more approachable. A lot of people now come up and tell me how much my work means to them. It's nice to know when you are appreciated.

Whether or not I'm appreciated, I'm not trying to make Pablum for the masses or lower the work down to a level to be appreciated by the great unwashed. Art requires work and you need to look at a lot of it. A work of art is like a vessel or a magic wand and each person can get a different substance out of that vessel. It's magic because one person's experience is going to be different from another's experience.

Nuance and subtlety come only after tremendous exposure to both art and music. It may even be truer with art because we can easily remember a tune and even the lyrics from when we were twelve years old. But most people's memory of visual information is very short – it dissipates, it leaves. It's like a bucket with a hole in it and you just have to keep putting water in, or it goes out the bottom as fast as it goes in.

So it's really important if you are interested in having any kind of sophistication in the visual arts to constantly immerse yourself in it. See as much as you can and know where the work fits into the larger picture of what's going on in the art world at this particular time. And that's hard work.

SPIKE LEE

Changing the filmmaking landscape

Spike Lee, the film director, producer, writer and actor, is noted for his movies about people and places, which examine race relations, urban crime and political issues. He heads a production company, a recording studio and a retail outlet, "Spike's Joint," for merchandise associated with his films. He also teaches film and established a minority scholarship at New York University's Tisch School of the Arts. He has written several books, produced music videos and produced and directed television commercials. He is known as one of the most original and innovative filmmakers in the world, presenting the different facets of black culture.

I think creativity is intuition, a gut feeling. The motivation for creativity is most often the need to express your ideas to other people.

Artists want to share their ideals, beliefs and viewpoints on the world with other human beings. It is hard for me to say that A-B-C-D is what a creative person does. What I do know is that a creative person is someone who is open-minded.

As an artist, you have to be open-minded, because when creativity comes to you – when the muse comes to you – you have to be receptive. Creative ideas don't come by appointment but come when they come, and you have to be ready when they visit.

> I think creativity is intuition, a gut feeling. The motivation for creativity is most often the need to express your ideas to other people.

Early on, I was able to remember a lot of ideas that would come to me when I was sleeping. Now I have to get up and write them down or I forget them. Sometimes I'm too lazy to get up in the middle of the night to write them down and I think I'll remember the ideas the next morning. But I've forgotten a lot of good stuff that way.

Creativity is something that not everybody has. Everybody has gifts, but creativity does not visit everybody. I think it's really something that is God-given. It can be honed, sharpened and developed – but you have to have that gift. The very fortunate people are those with parents who recognize that their children have gifts and they support and encourage them to develop.

Spike Lee at one of the locations from the documentary on Hurricane Katrina.
Courtesy of 40 Acres and a Mule Filmworks

My creative background

My father is a musician and my mother was an art teacher. I was a really late developer. I didn't know that I wanted to be a filmmaker until the summer between my sophomore and junior years at Morehouse College in Atlanta, Georgia. But once I knew it was what I wanted to do, I just made sure that everything I did would go toward that goal of being a filmmaker.

I can't discount the fact that my mother used to take me to movies all the time at a very early age. She would also take me to Broadway plays. And I saw my father play at the Village Vanguard, or at the The Bitter End. Sometimes he played at the Newport Jazz Festival with people like Odetta, Judy Collins and Josh White. He's the bass player on that Peter Paul and Mary record, *Puff the Magic Dragon.*

In retrospect, I see that my siblings and I were exposed to the arts at a very, very early age, and that's why my sister is an actress, and my brother is a photographer. I can definitely trace that back to the fact that we grew up in a house where there was an appreciation of the arts. My parents never drummed into our heads that, "You have to do something that's going to make money," and we were never discouraged from developing our creative instincts.

A lot of parents crush their children's dreams. I give many lectures at universities and colleges all over the country, and always say that parents kill more dreams than anybody. They squash any artistic drive that children have when they say, "We don't want you doing this stuff, because you can't make money and you'll end up being a cab driver or a waitress."

This can be devastating. I don't know how you recover from that if you have a great love of the arts. You'll end up hating your parents for that, especially when you're stuck in some dead-end job doing something that you really hate.

I also got my work ethic from my parents, especially my mother, who did not tolerate anything I did that was substandard. She did not like any half-stepping or hanging around aimlessly and wanted you to do your best all the time. Being young at that time, I thought that she was picking on me.

> ... we have made a film every year and that makes twenty films in twenty years.

From my father, I probably get my stubbornness. He still refuses, to this day, to play *electric* bass. Anything electronic has no use to him. The sad thing, or the lucky thing, for him is that he had a wife who, once he made that decision, supported him. My mother had to start working again because, with a wife and five kids, my father made the decision that, "I'm not going to play electric bass, and if we have to starve, we're going to starve." I hope I'll never be put in that position, where I have to do *Rocky 8* so that my kids will eat.

Scene with Denzel Washington portraying Malcolm X in the 1992 movie. *Courtesy of 40 Acres and a Mule Filmworks*

After graduating high school, I went to Morehouse College from 1975 to 1979 and got a B.A. in mass communications. Then I applied to the three top film schools: the University of Califorinia (UCLA) and the University of South California (USC), both in Los Angeles, and New York University (NYU). I didn't get a high enough score to get into USC and UCLA. But since you didn't have to take the Graduate Record Examination to get into NYU, I got in there.

I spent three years at NYU and my piece won the student academy award. It took another three years, into 1986, to shoot *She's Gotta Have It*. Since 1986, we have made a film every year and that makes twenty films in twenty years. From the beginning, it was our ambition, our goal, to build up a body of work.

I like to organize

Film was the area I was most suited for. In film you have *all* the arts to work with – dance, music and photography – a perfect fit for me.

I like working with the team but I am also a leader. When I was younger, I was always the organizer for teams on my block – stickball, two-man touch and basketball. Even in college, when there was no intramural softball, I said one day, "Let's start a team." I started a league and I was the commissioner.

> … I do believe the audiences want to see fresh, new work, and not necessarily another comic book, or an old TV show, or a sequel that the studios seem to make with more regularity than ever before.

I love all sports. I love going to games and I love to play softball and tennis. I have season tickets to the New York Knicks basketball games. My son also loves sports. Yesterday, he had a soccer game in the morning at Chelsea Piers and a Little League baseball game in the afternoon. So I get great joy watching my son play there.

A lot of my inspiration really has come from athletes, such as Willie Mays, Muhammad Ali, John Thompson, Tommy Smith, John Carlos, Jackie Robinson, Joe Louis and Walt Frazier. They were athletes, not filmmakers, and they were my heroes growing up. And Michael Jordan's a good friend.

I also love music, any kind of music. How you can you top hearing Beethoven or Stevie Wonder or Duke Ellington? In high school I remember listening to Stevie Wonder's albums and, later on, listening to Prince. Words, sculpture and paintings are great, but I think that talent is God-given, and when God gives out the talent and the gifts, musicians get the most. That is why I have always felt that musicians were the greatest artists. Other people might feel differently, but for me they are the greatest.

Music is a very important part of my films. I know many top musicians who I think are wonderful. I never would have expected it, but with the development of my career I'm now able to work with these artists. That's the great thing about being a filmmaker.

Making the films

I love being a filmmaker and a film director. I grew up in Brooklyn and I was the firstborn. So perhaps I learned to be a leader and an organizer because I was the oldest. I haven't made a study of it but perhaps being a leader results from being the oldest sibling in a family.

This comes in handy if you want to be a leader in filmmaking. We directors have to answer a thousand questions, because people look to the director for, "Which way are we going to go? What lens? What's this? Do we move the camera?" You constantly get questions like that. Someone should do a study on how many questions are given to a director on an average twelve-hour day.

To be honest, we have always tried to make entertaining films that are not mindless entertainment. I think that a film can be entertaining and also have some serious thought behind it. Look at *Inside Man* – by mid-2006 that film had made over $85 million domestically and $75 million internationally. It's an entertaining film, but very intelligent too.

I feel that it's very hard to do both things, but when you do them well, audiences appreciate it. And I do believe the audiences want to see fresh, new work, and not necessarily another comic book, or an old TV show, or a sequel that the studios seem to make with more regularity than ever before.

I go anywhere and everywhere for new ideas. Ideas just don't reside in one remote area. They are everywhere. I don't always write the script. For instance, the script for *Inside Man* was written by a very fine, first time screenwriter, Russell Gurwitz. I was slipped a copy of that script, read it and liked it very much.

She's Gotta Have It was my first feature film. That was twenty years ago. Wow! I was three years out of NYU graduate film school and just trying to get something made. It was shot in black and white in twelve days. No budget. I just winged it.

Dance hall scene from the 1999 film, *Summer of Sam. Courtesy of 40 Acres and a Mule Filmworks*

Do the Right Thing was my third film, and I had the title before I had anything else. Then I decided that it should take place on one block in Brooklyn, New York, on the hottest day of the summer. It's been documented that, in New York City, the murder rate and domestic disputes go up after 95° F heat. A fender bender could turn into somebody getting shot just because of the heat.

At the time we shot the film – under the reign of New York's Mayor Ed Koch – races in the city were polarized, and I wanted to use that. Historically there has always been a beef between Italian-Americans and African-Americans. I wanted to use that too. And it was also around the time of the racially charged Tawana Brawley controversy.

We knew that if we shot the film that summer, it would come out the following summer, right before the primary election battle between Mayor Koch and David Dinkins. *Do the Right Thing* had many references to registering to vote in it, and we had things like "Dump Koch" spray-painted on walls in the background!

I write my own stuff, and even the scripts that I do not write are still a reflection of things that I've done. I've written *She's Gotta Have It*, *School Daze*, *Do the Right Thing*, *Mo' Better Blues*, *Jungle Fever* and *Bamboozle*. I've also written scripts with other people. I co-wrote *Malcolm X*.

What I like about film is the entire process. I came up with the title for *Do the Right Thing* one day and a year later it was a finished product. The exciting thing is to go through this whole process. People keep mentioning I should do a Broadway show. A musical of *Do the Right Thing* or something like that. It would be interesting.

I think that a lot of creative ideas have to do with ego. There are times where suggestions come from other sources and if an idea is good, we'll go with it. It's not productive for me to reject an idea just because I didn't come up with it. I have to do what's best for the project, and I can't come up with every idea. So I rely upon my cinematographer. I rely upon my composer, my editor, my costume designer and my production designer, and professionals in related fields, so long as we all have the same vision.

> My job is to gather everybody together and say we're going in this or that direction.

The original idea for *Crooklyn* came from my sister, Juaux, and brother, David. *Summer of Sam* came from Michael Imperioli and Victor Colicchio. I wrote *Clockers* based on a script by Richard Price. I wrote *Malcolm X* based on a script by James Baldwin and Arnold Pearl.

My job is to gather everybody together and say we're going in this or that direction. But they are the experts in their fields and they know more than I know in those fields. So I'm cool with that.

I'm especially proud of my recent documentary about New Orleans and the Katrina disaster – *When the Levies Broke* – which is very strong. It was shown on HBO on the first anniversary of Katrina. The film runs in two segments, each four hours.

The only sports film we made was called *He Got Game*, which I wrote and which starred Denzel Washington. Denzel plays an ex-convict who is let out of prison and convinces his son, the best high school player in the nation, to go to a specific school. It's one of the four films that I've done with Denzel, the others are *Mo' Better Blues*, *Malcolm X*, and *Inside Man*.

> I think we've really changed the landscape as far as African-Americans and minorities are concerned.

It's not just fun and games

While the first step in making a movie is deciding on the story you want to tell, the hard part is always getting the financing. A painter just needs paint, a canvas and some brushes. You need a lot more than that to do a film.

Sometimes the financing is independent and sometimes you're working with a studio. I've done both. My latest film, *Inside Man*, is for Universal Pictures. I have done six films for Universal Pictures – *Do the Right Thing*, *Mo' Better Blues*, *Jungle Fever*, *Clockers*, *Crooklyn* and *Inside Man*.

Those financing the film sometimes, though not always, try to influence the direction. People want to have their opinions heard, and I understand that. But I have final cut.

I don't have final cut in commercials and I understand that going in. Commercials can be very creative or they can be very stupid. You just have to be lucky and get a client who is open to creativity. Most clients say they want creative work but they actually want the same old rigmarole, just spiced up a little.

Some commercials can be so redundant. What are you going to do with toilet paper? An agency might come to me, knowing that I'm creative, but that doesn't mean that they are going to let me open up. There are parameters and you have the leash on.

You can't always talk them into being creative because people get paralyzed when decisions can affect their job. So everything is close to the vest and they're just trying to save their necks.

I've also run into this in the studio system. I think people who have no vision are the biggest drag. They just can't see anything really creative. I don't want to make it too personal, but I think that lack of vision is one of the biggest problems in the world, not only with creativity, but also with a whole myriad of things.

Spike Lee (left) and actor Mekhi Phifer at film location. *Courtesy of 40 Acres and a Mule Filmworks*

And the client test markets everything. They assume that Joe Blow, who they pick off the street to be in the focus group, knows everything. They automatically accept that the most outspoken person in the focus group speaks for Joe America and knows what he is talking about. You are sunk because they believe it's the gospel. It happens all the time.

Awards are nice but ...

As I said before, creative people want to share their ideas with other people. Whether they do so because they crave professional recognition, or whether they create just for personal satisfaction depends on the individual. As for me, I just want to do the work.

Being in the film business, I have learned very early on that you can be put in a very difficult spot if you allow any group to sanction your work. You cannot let somebody else validate your work, whether it's the Academy of Motion Picture Arts and Sciences, or whoever. You have to validate yourself, especially when your film doesn't receive nominations or awards, or similar recognition.

I've never made a film – and I hope I never will – where we go in saying, "Let's go for an Academy Award on this. We're going for a nomination on this one." We don't think like that and we don't operate like that. I don't know how it would do you any good if you thought that way.

There's nothing wrong with saying that you want to get on the map and make a name for yourselves with a film. We did that with *She's Gotta Have It*, my first film, and this year is that film's twentieth anniversary. We said at the time that we wanted that film to make a name for ourselves. But that is totally different from saying that we want to win an Academy Award or a nomination.

The impact of my movies

I'm not going to say that my movies have changed people's ways of thinking. Somebody else will have to say that. But I think that we have made an impact in these last twenty years.

When I say *we*, I am talking about a collective *we*, meaning all the people who have worked together on these films. I think we've really changed the landscape as far as African-Americans and minorities are concerned – not only in front of the camera but, maybe more importantly, behind the camera.

With every film, we made sure that there was representation of African-Americans and minorities behind the camera. These were qualified people, but historically they had been shunted from the unions.

We always hope that our films that address specific issues will provoke conversation and dialogue. They don't have to be influential but just stimulate discussion. I could not get a higher compliment than when people, after they see one of my movies – *Do the Right Thing*, or *Jungle Fever*, or *Malcolm X*, or even *Inside Man* – are talking about the film in the lobby. If my film provoked discussion, I think I have made something worthwhile.

CHRIS BANGLE

Creating the personification of BMW Group design

Chris Bangle is BMW Group chief of design and has been credited with the achievement of making BMWs stand out from the pack. Within the BMW Group, he is responsible for design within all brands, BMW, MINI and Rolls-Royce. He began his career at Opel, and then moved to Fiat, where he became chief designer of Fiat Centro Stile. He joined BMW in 1992, their first American chief of design. To many, the styling for BMW represents a move into the future for what had been considered stolidly conservative cars and, among BMW fans, there has been a vocal debate concerning this change of style.

Creative people are driven by factors of validation and a sense of acknowledgment. That does not mean they need a third party to do the acknowledging. Often it can be a dialogue only between the designer and the creation, but this needs to be a loop of personal satisfaction to the tune of: "I came, I Designed, You Exist." The bigger the loop and the more people that enter into it, the more energy a creative person is usually rewarded with.

What separates creative people from merely effervescent people is that they have to do *something* – they actually have to bring into existence what did not exist before. To them, creativity is not just an intellectual exercise, it's a process that ends as some sort of tangible product, whether it's writing, a piece of artwork, an object, or a statement – something that they can go back and refer to.

Creative people are "doers"

I can remember when I attended art class in college we would argue for a whole session over "What is Art?" Someone suggested, "It's something you *do* and not something you just talk about." I agree completely.

Since art and design are about actually making something, I work at developing my own theories on how this "making" relates to the world around us … how to get particular aspects of life to come together in a more succinct manner, to design their relationship – that is what design skills enable. And I

Chris Bangle. *Courtesy of BMW AG*

would argue that there is an "energy gain" in that. It's thrilling to see things come together, to create a new "whole." Even though it might be easier for nature to let all the beans roll downhill and disperse themselves, there's something to be gained by being able to have those beans organized in just a particular manner. I think the universe gives that energy back to you and you feel good about yourself. Designers would have never conceived of the second law of thermodynamics!

Growing up making things

As a kid, I was raised in a very "doing" environment. My parents were active in different types of social functions, but they were also the kind of people who were always busy in the workshop making something. My siblings and I were obligated to make things, particularly at Christmas! Store-bought gifts were the exception.

My father worked for a lumber company and kept a "doing" environment going – lots of tools and equipment around to work with wood. Otherwise my parents were not big on painting-type artwork, so I didn't grow up wielding a brush in my crib. All my visualization skills such as cartooning came later and were only a sideline as I went through high school and then into college, where I planned to become a Methodist minister.

My father had learned surveying in his college days, and encouraged my interest in technical drafting and calligraphy. He bought me pens and a lettering book when I was an adolescent, and I even lettered the confirmation names in the bibles for our church! In high school I took classes in the graphic arts, learning to run stat cameras and printing presses. It was all great fun and quite a background for my design studies later.

How I became a car designer

As one could imagine, design school was an environment that was not so foreign to me: tool shops, technical drawing, model making. It was, however, very demanding, and not at all like normal college in its pace and stress levels.

I learned my basic design skills at the Art Center College of Design in California. But to me, a far more important phase of my professional career was the two years before that when I went to the University of Wisconsin, Marathon County. There I had truly inspiring and talented teachers. At the time, I took classes that seemed the correct prerequisite for seminary – philosophy, psychology, literature and history, as opposed to the hard sciences or mathematics. Later, when I became a design manager, that knowledge of the humanities became especially useful. A big company has its personal traits and "ticks" just like a real person. And a car is also very much like a person, *and its design is the outward expression of its character*.

What I learned in college has helped me a great deal, giving me particular insights into how to approach problems. It also turns out that my study of creative writing and literature has been extremely helpful in design because the creative process of designing a car is very similar to writing a story; with the work of a design manager like that of an editor. The same basic steps are at work, which is something I didn't know then but am thankful for having learned first on paper – where the "editing" is cheaper than in clay!

Growing up

At our house there was already always something happening related to cars, such as a slot car set that I had as a kid – as you might expect, my father and I made a big one from wood after I drew the technical drawing! When I was six years old he brought home a recording of the 1963 Watkins Glen races; nothing but engine sounds zooming by and an announcer belting out names like Stirling Moss. I would play this on the record player for hours – this was the coolest thing! Ours was the kind of neighborhood where the kids were always making their own go-karts out of wood, rolling them down the hills. We progressed on to real cars, and it was natural to take them apart, fiddle and put them together and try to get them to work.

> ... a car is also very much like a person, and its design is the outward expression of its character.

But I didn't come across the idea that car design as a profession until much later, when I was about ready to go to college. I discovered that there was a college called Art Center College of Design, in Pasadena, California, and I visited the school since my sister lived not far away from it.

During the two years that I was doing pre-seminary studies at the University of Wisconsin, I started thinking about car design and I created a portfolio that eventually led to my acceptance at the Art Center. So, as they say, instead of going into religion, I joined "the other side," working for the "dark side of the force!"

A car is like a person

A car is more than just a set of geometries that are hung together around a group of functions. It is a creation with a character, personification in a dynamic, useful object. And as always, it is a statement – an expression of the intention of the engineers as they put together its fundamental architecture.

The product semanticists define design as: "Design equals Meaning." No

Studio design development of the BMW X5. *Courtesy of BMW AG*

meaning, no design. Pure art may have implied or discovered meanings, but the purposefulness of design requires meaning to be built into its visible justification, its reason for being addressing the function in question. The interpreting and planning of meaning in physical objects requires some understanding of human relationships – they work well as metaphors. And in the same way that character assessment establishes a hypothetical ideal against which we measure our own performance, sanity and healthiness, there are also ideals in the character reference of car design. Why is one car considered successful and another is not? What is beauty? Is it merely a shape, or does it also have to do with the reflection of the inner soul? Is there value beyond just the skin? Where does one turn to for answers to these questions?

> Why is one car considered successful and another is not? What is beauty? Is it merely a shape, or does it also have to do with the reflection of the inner soul?

The best book I have ever read on car design is Sir Kenneth Clark's *The Nude*. I have two editions of it, one filled with notes and drawings. When I first got hold of the book a few years ago, I went through it and crossed out the word "nude" and wrote in the word "car." As you follow Clark's analysis of how artists have tried to interpret the many values of human expression through their renditions of "The Nude," you realize that it is an exact parallel to what we are trying to do with a car's design.

Other car designers may share this viewpoint, but I would hesitate to speak for them. We are a closed shop even among ourselves– and don't talk too much outside our own culture. We don't publish peer review journals about our work, and we don't hold car design conferences to exchange treatises on why we do what we do. Car design per se is very much a private sort of guild. You will find many books on *design* and books on *cars* in the stores, but very few if at all on *car design*.

The car *industry* is another story. Because it has much to do with economic factors, mass employment and the technologies of production, it tends to open itself up for that type of analysis, dialogue and discussion. We have no problem discussing the *industry*. But car *design* is considered a mysterious black box even by people who have been in the industry for their entire lives.

Working at the BMW Group

Being a design director in a car company is truly like being married to a perpetually pregnant wife. Something is always about to be born. Car design directors are the worst people to convince to take vacation time. They never want to leave the studio because they are afraid they will miss some important change. In gestation every minute is precious. Something is happening – your wife is changing, her glow is changing, the baby is changing – *you* are changing. And as we all know, if you just step away from your wife's side, even for even a short time, inevitably that is when the baby does its first kick – and you've missed it.

It is like that with the car and motorcycle models that I see on the studio plates – every day they're different. Constant change *is* the constant, and if you suddenly go off on vacation, when you come back there is the risk of the surprise: "Whoa! What happened?"

> "An automobile is what I use, a car is what I am."

Like mothers and fathers around their babies, there is a huge amount of pride and identification in our work. People inside BMW are very passionate about cars, and they certainly feel that their product is a personification of their work that has gone into it. BMW is blessed with what is perhaps the highest employee to product identity of any company you can think of. You wouldn't get that emotion if the product were an impersonal object or just a representation of a particular set of perform-ance curves. You only get that feeling if you can say, "This car is *me*."

Some years ago, when we were discussing the difference between the word "car" and "automobile" in the English language, a woman said to me, "An auto-mobile is what I use, a car is what I am." Ever since then we have used this simple description to separate what makes a BMW special, different from a mass-produced, non-premium product. Others are making automobiles that you use – we are making *cars* that are an expression of yourself. Just think about the word "automobile" – "auto" means that something operates by itself and "mobile" means that it moves. Given that definition, even an elevator is an "automobile." And who wants to identify with an elevator?

How ideas develop

Ideas and the flow of ideas are important, and I've found that ideas flow with me and with the people in the team when they are *enabled*. "Enabling" is not "care-taking" or "protecting." Enabling means providing the means for an idea to propagate, to grow. Some people protect their ideas so much they never seem to have another. Of course, for a company where selling ideas is a service, that sort of husbanding may make sense, but in a production house where ideas are the route to the product, you need to energize and activate the causal idea chain.

If an *individual* stops and gets focused on a particular idea too long, the channel of creating other ideas gets stopped too. Enabling stops. But if you open up and let others in on it, it might generate more ideas. I don't worry about letting someone else take my idea and run with it, because I know there will be

BMW concept car. *Courtesy of BMW AG*

another idea coming along for me to think about. I like the unconventional concepts and being in the feedback loop of generating new thoughts and awareness with my team, improving my insights with their inputs.

Creativity as a team process

Here at BMW I consider myself just one part of the catalytic effect. In chemistry it takes more than one molecule to achieve a reaction. You need a "soup" already primed with the components in place for change and the common "will" to see it through, in this case a corporate will.

In a company like BMW, creativity is a team process and the design director's role is not to stand in front and say, "I did this and I did that." That may work elsewhere, but not in our design culture. Rather, my job is one of making sure there is a consistent design strategy that we are following and that the criteria have been discussed between the board and the designers in a manner that is always clear, correct and coherent. None of this is a given and all of it must be crafted and tuned to keep a relevancy alive and a vision flowing. Usually this involves no small amount of drawing to make it happen. Sometimes it requires me to pen graphs and charts on napkins to show relationships between phenomena, sometimes I need to be able to quickly sketch a fender or a high-light or a detail so that everyone involved knows where the issue is at. Common understanding is what I'm trying to achieve.

> When, out of all this competition, we come to the conclusion that this is the car design that we want, it's done as a matter of conviction.

To get a design off the paper and into production one quickly discovers is not a given, it is something that you have to fight for. It's not always easy for people to understand the relationship between technical decisions made at this point in time on a project and what will happen because of the aesthetics at a later time. You have to make causal links clear and continuously reinforce the fact that what we're all trying to achieve is better served if we make one set of decisions as opposed to another.

This is truly the job of design management, and *Fight for Design* is a fundamental building block of our design group. But the goal is not to block the correct solution because artists are stubborn, rather to find the right set of priorities. I would always use that word over "compromise," which implies winners and losers. Design is so subjective that you cannot assume it will get a fair hearing in a debate with rational and objective counterarguments, but good design management shows its added value by protecting the design from unintended harm.

What one protects one had better get to know, and car design is an emotion-ally visual type of knowledge. When dealing with a designer's sketches or their model, a director needs to bring a fresh set of eyes to what everyone has been looking at. Designers themselves can be handicapped by their closeness to the problem at hand. There is a time axis of understanding involved in "seeing;" the secret is to be able to project your assessment forward: "How will this look to me in five years?"

In car design, the pluses and minuses of a surface are sometimes measured in the thousandths of a millimeter, and at a certain point, one thousandth of a millimeter too much. This is not something evident at a quick glance. I cannot just walk into the studio and say, "Well, it looks okay to me," and then walk away. Designers respect you when you respect their work, and give it the time needed to work on your emotions.

There is a culture of "seeing" in car design that is unlike any other business that I know, perhaps because the scale and surface qualities involved are so unique. Architecture and fashion are not concerned with "perfect surfaces," but we are. Product design may specify perfect surfaces, but never at the scale or emotional dynamic level that cars work at. This is a special facet of the job that also bonds the designers with the modelers in an almost Zen-like state of suspension. Finding the time for this is truly one of my greatest management challenges, but the rewards are beautiful, if, I'm afraid, not very explainable! But after twenty odd years, my wife has learned to expect me home late with the only explanation, "Sorry, looking at a model."

How we carry out our ideas

There are three phases in design at BMW that we go through. We call the first phase *Understanding* – which means that, as a first step, you have to understand clearly what you want to do.

The next phase is *Believing*. This means that you have selected the one design from all the various choices with no real objective proof that it is right, but your knowledge-based intuition tells you that you must proceed with that solution, and only that one.

The third and final phase is called *Seeing* – which means you have really got to look at your chosen model and refine it, to take care of the little fine-grain issues, to make sure any blemishes are gone so that the final product is perfect.

The car business is a very competitive business and we have design teams compete against one another. When, out of all this competition, we come to the conclusion that this is the car design that we want, it's done as a matter of conviction. There's no statistical proof. There is no way to go out and test what will be valid in four years from now when it comes on the market. Believing has to come from within, because management has understood the problems, the brand and the crucial issues behind this particular car. The experience of the final product is understood and accepted as its own authentic character, and with that a commitment to the character of the brand itself is made.

Each one of these phases takes us a year. It takes us a year to *understand* what needs to be done, a year to *believe* that this is the right choice, and a year to *look at it* and make sure it comes out perfect.

Around the car industry there is often talk about reducing "time to market." This can be done in lots of ways, but it's very difficult to tell somebody to take 20 percent out of their time of *understanding*. Or speed up their *believing*. Or can you *see* faster? It is a human timescale that we're working with, and that's

BMW Group Designworks USA, Hospitality Lounge designed to be taken down and rebuilt within three days. *Courtesy of BMW AG*

why, for a process as complicated as a car, it takes about a year to go through each one of the three steps. If you try to skip a stage, my experience says you will be doomed to repeat it later, when it really gets expensive!

Our creative breakthrough at BMW

The creative breakthrough that led to the design change at BMW was really a very simple, straightforward process. This is an organization that looks downstream a long way to plot its course. And managing car design has been compared to piloting a supertanker. You can make a tiny "two degrees of rudder" change upstream in the process now and inevitably seven years downstream when the car comes into the market, the "ship" has moved in a big arc, perhaps away from your original goal.

So in the very much "upstream" concept phase, BMW management asked my team to assess where this was all taking us. If we keep doing what we are doing, what are we going to have "downstream" a few years from now?

It didn't take too long to realize that there were some serious limitations in our design philosophy and how we had been approaching aesthetic relationships. We were truly approaching problem solving with a single-solution mentality that allowed us to do extremely high-quality variations on a theme, but did not allow us to introduce new themes. And as long as we were doing one kind of car in different sizes, that approach was pretty much okay. But times were changing.

The BMW 3 Series, 5 Series and 7 Series cars are similar types of sport salons, just in different formats. A similar design approach was not difficult. But that was not helping us with new vehicles called the X5 and X3, the Z3 and the Z4. And what is a 1 Series? A small 3 Series? These projects were all on the horizon and we knew that we would have to fit them into a coherent BMW design philosophy. This was not a simple exercise in scaling.

> This new car was for us the biggest technical jump we had ever made in a single generation change.

We presented an alternative to the board, a spectrum approach using the 7 Series as the crucial starting point. This was not because we thought the 7 Series was the best one to start with, but, for timing, it was the next player at bat.

This new car was for us the biggest technical jump we had ever made in a single generation change. It involved more performance and feature improvements and innovations than ever before. We brought this new personality together into a product that leveraged a whole new design philosophy and, at the same time, extended the earlier one. The product character was new, fresh, exciting and not without controversy, but over time has proved to be the global solution.

I predicted that the clarity of the solutions on the 7 Series would find their way into other cars when they confronted the same problems we had, and sure enough there have been a number of signs that our lead has its followers. Sometimes it is easy to forget that form really does follow function, and the forces that we contended with are not ours alone to confront. We now have the best-selling 7 Series ever and that's a nice "happy ending" to any story!

How I look for ideas

I keep an open mind, a messy desk, stuff on the walls and a full calendar of people I don't know who are coming to talk to me. I tend to open myself up to things rather than close myself away, which doesn't get my mail answered so speedily but does keep me inspired.

Like any designer, I take notes on what I see and think and make a lot of drawings. I fill my sketchbooks on what I see in life, what I think of and what I hear. I often sketch an idea that I think relates to something important at the moment and then go back into the sketchbooks to refresh myself years later. I don't claim to have such a good brain capacity to be able to load all this stuff on my own hard drive and pull it up at will. I need that paper in front of me. For me, my sketchbooks are a very important part of keeping my creative process running.

These sketches are not necessarily cars or people – they are about everything, and I keep a sketchbook with me all the time. My wife is happy because she knows I am never bored. While she shops or does something, I will just pull out a sketchbook and draw a lamppost or something else I see. This will lead to another inspiration, sometime, somehow, and even if it is just honing my art skills, it is a joy.

Creating an emotional message

A favorite project that I was involved in from day one as the main creative focus was for Munich's Pinakothek der Moderne, a museum that I understand houses the world's largest collection of design and applied arts. BMW Group design was asked if we could create a permanent installation for the brand new museum building, on a wall that was 12 meters tall and 14 meters wide. It was to represent a synthesis of the dynamic between engineers and designers, between car design and the rest of the world of design, and between the personal emotions of a car designer and his work. Oh, and we had to do it in three months!

I put a "war room" office in place right next to mine, brought in four people who I considered my most creative, gave them a vision and set them at work creating things that I could go next door and react to.

My concern was with the holistic experience of being a car designer, and the goal was to bring every visitor into that role, even if only for a moment. I drew heavily from relationships of truth, beauty and love that I had learned in my literature classes, fundamental messages of poetry and expressionism that came through the written word. I wanted a similar content – What is truth? What is beauty? What is love? – but in the context of the car and its designer. These are the components of the platonic ideal of art and the title of the installation became *The Art of Car Design*.

I did my own sketches, collected my own samples of reference work on it, and threw them at the team, and they threw back at me their interpretation of it all. By the end of a few weeks, we had something that the five of us felt really comfortable about expressing. We focused on the tensions and emotions of artistic creation in the paradigm of car design, the role of the past, the individual, the rules of the real world, and the secret desires of the inner ego.

With a tiny scale model and fifteen minutes to explain what we were up to, I presented the concept to the BMW board, and got their approval. Amazingly, we built it in the remaining fifty days and had it ready for the museum's opening. *The Art of Car Design* installation contains about thirty-five tons of marble, and another twenty-five tons of steel, plaster and car parts, and is a permanent piece in the Pinakothek der Moderne's Neue Sammlung design exhibition.

Seeing it today, I am still impressed by the work of the team. It's extremely well organized so that despite its scale and level of abstraction, the image that comes across is not one of man and society, or about women and children or war or religion. It is about car designers and engineers and their product in the real world.

In all, it was a wonderful experience with beautiful collaborators, and one of the most emotional pieces I ever worked on. And, in that way, it closes the loop on my personal learning curve from pre-seminary college through my car industry experience. I'm proud of my contribution to its existence and that I have the good fortune to work for a company that could understand and prioritize such a creation.

PAUL WARWICK THOMPSON

Looking for enduring significance

Paul Warwick Thompson is the director of the Smithsonian's Cooper-Hewitt, National Design Museum, which he joined after serving as the director of the Design Museum in London. Born and educated in the United Kingdom, he started as a scriptwriter and researcher for the Design Council, a government organization promoting design in British industry. He is the first non-American to serve as director in Cooper-Hewitt's history, where his responsibilities are the organization of industrial design exhibits. His aspiration is to capture the imagination and create a long-ranging interest in industrial design among an audience of all ages and walks of life.

I think creativity is an attribute that many people possess in very different ways. Creativity can manifest itself in the most humdrum approach toward solving a problem, such as finding a very simple solution to something that causes a blockage between two people or between two inanimate objects – a very simple solution to what otherwise would be an impasse.

And then, at the other end of the scale, when you think of the creativity of a genius such as Mozart, who composed symphonies at the age of seven, and you try to find what makes a genius, the whole idea of creativity appears like some God-given gift.

In our design world, we tend to think about creativity as people who have created something that has extraordinary visual delight, or something with commercial application that has incredible appeal.

Take, for example, a person like Frank Gehry, the architect. I suspect that he is somebody who is really not bound by convention, whose mind is really racing with all possibilities and is not being bound by either structural or formal conventions. You have to expect that when somebody is so ahead of his time, he has to be a maverick, full of vigor and a bit of an outsider, not part of the establishment. It takes that voice in the wilderness, the sort of a maverick like Gehry to be recognized as a creative genius.

Paul Warwick Thompson. *Courtesy of Cooper-Hewitt, National Design Museum*

Thoughts about creative people

Creative people in a particular mold are often viewed as being different from other people. They are seen by many people as being either loners or individuals who, having an artistic temperament, are not the easiest to work with. There are lots of clichés that can be put around creative people, but I don't know whether all creative people fit into that mold.

There are many differences in how creative people see themselves. Some believe that they are involved in creative activities because they feel that they are not good in anything else. They are very monodimensional. They know that they are good at being a botanist, or a rocket engineer, and they are going have to stick to that forever. Others feel just the opposite – that they can do everything.

> There's nothing at the human life level that's more fundamental than being a fantastic parent.

I suspect that as we map more and more of the brain and the genes, we'll learn more about creativity from a physiological point of view. We'll probably find that there is a part of the brain that has particular cognitive faculties. There may be a more physiological interpretation of what creativity is. I'm not saying that this will reduce creativity to some sort of clinical formula, but I think that it will have a bearing upon how we look at creativity and creative individuals.

Creative people are naturally inquisitive and exploring, and so they are always going to be making discoveries leading to inventions and finding uncharted territory. I think this is a very involuntary reflex action. I do not think that most creative people can help themselves from being creative. I think this is something that you are born with. It can be trained to a certain extent, but you are not likely to succeed if you were not initially born with an integral need to create something.

It matters not whether you want to compose a fabulous piece of music, start a theater company, or create a visual motif that's going to be used in an advertising campaign – you are looking at things and putting them together in your mind in a way that others cannot.

Creativity within an individual can manifest itself in many different ways such as in somebody actually being an amazingly good parent. There's nothing at the human life level that's more fundamental than being a fantastic parent. That's the ultimate – that's probably the most creative act.

A creative person could be an incredibly good homemaker. Or you could see a pattern of creativity in somebody who is initially trained as a draftsman or as an artist, but becomes a photographer and eventually a moviemaker. People's creativity can bend and be reformed by circumstance, and adapt along the way to whatever a particular set of circumstances demands.

The *Fashion in Colors* exhibition explored color as a design element through 300 years of western clothing.
Courtesy of Cooper-Hewitt

Very often the most creative people are thought to be innovators. But you don't necessarily have to be an innovator to be creative. People can do some extraordinary things in landscape design that may not be very innovative, but it's still remarkably creative.

This goes for fashion design as well. I can think of fashion designers who are not innovators but whom I would still describe as being very creative individuals. Designers who have an instinctive feel for cut, volume, shape and what makes people comfortable may create clothes that may not be totally innovative, but are still creatively exciting.

Some creative people apply their skills and learning so that they are able to leap from one discipline to another. This is a curious aspect of creativity and there are many interesting examples of this. For example, Chekhov was a doctor, and also a fabulous playwright. We did an exhibition in 2004 on Christopher Dresser who trained as a botanist and then became an industrial designer.

It's very interesting to see the way that exceptional individuals, who may well be creative, tend not to view things in distinct, discrete boxes. There is a breadth of vision to exceptional individuals where they can cross boundaries from medicine to playwriting, or from botany to industrial design, not seeing things locked up as two different, discrete cultures, science and the arts.

Another example of an exceptionally diverse design individual is Giovanni

Piranesi, who was an etcher, archaeologist and architect in the eighteenth century. Here again was somebody who was as at home with the fantastical as he was with the built, somebody who was not time bound by either conventions or boundaries or disciplines.

Piranesi was also a wonderful draftsman. His architectural drawings are fantastic. He's been put into art shows as a draftsman, rather than as a tremendous architect. Here is a creative genius that could look at different influences from the past and from a certain height to see things in that overarching manner, adapt them and create something new for his day.

How I came to become a creative administrator

I am from the United Kingdom and have always been interested in the performing arts, the visual arts and design and architecture.

I derive a special sense of pleasure from the arts. I'm interested in anything that results from creative acts – even cooking and gardening. I get a huge amount of personal fulfillment, intellectual stimulation and spiritual succor from being near great works of art, visiting museums, going to the theater, going to movies, going to historic houses, looking at contemporary architecture, collecting art. I've also enjoyed reading a huge amount of great literature. All these have been and still are my hobbies.

Both my parents were scientists, so they were creative people in their own way, but they were less interested in music or visual and literary arts. But I've always been very interested in visual culture. I always knew that I was going to work in the arts and as an arts administrator. Of course, at the age of eighteen or twenty, I was not quite sure whether I would be working for a ballet company or a museum, but I knew that I wanted to work in the arts.

I went to Bryanston School in Dorset, a school that produced Terence Conran, Lucien Freud and Howard Hodgkin. It was one of those schools that, from the 1920s to the 1950s, always meant to be a place that put great emphasis on creativity, whereas other schools were focused on academics. It was a private boarding school that prided itself on instruction in the visual and performing arts, and putting them on an equal footing with academic subjects.

However, by the time I went to the school in the 1970s, the world had changed. These days, everything is so much more vocationally driven and we place so much more emphasis on academic subjects than we do on practical skills. I can remember that, until the age of about fifteen, I had to study technical drawing, even though I never wanted to be a designer, and I never wanted to go and work in the metalworking shop. But the school insisted that everybody should learn technical drawing. It was very much part of the school's ethos that you value people who *make things*.

And so we had sculpture classes, pottery classes, technical drawing and studio art. It was a very privileged educational environment, but it was one where you would be left out if you were not "taking part."

The school was very proud of its alumni by pointing to the achievements of the classes from the 1930s to the 1960s, but I think that we, who graduated in the 1970s, were probably not its best crop.

I'm not a creative person in terms of being an artist or a designer. My role is that of an administrator – to interpret and edit the works to others and to create interesting exhibits, rather than creating any art or design of my own. This is very much a creative endeavor in its own way.

Creating an exhibition

When we do an exhibition at the Cooper-Hewitt, National Design Museum, it has to be a topic that has got some longevity to it. There are moments with certain exhibitions where you want to present what is happening now. You may want to give a snapshot of the moment, or a snapshot of a past moment. But what you are always looking for is a feeling of enduring significance; something that you hope will still resonate with people twenty years hence. What you hope is that people will look at the exhibition catalog and say, "You know, I learned so much from that exhibition. It was such a defining exhibition in my own personal creative development, my own understanding of design history."

Every exhibition will not always have that educative long-term impact. It would be fantastic if this could be achieved.

Creating an exhibition is like assembling any creative team you want to bring together. It is sort of the equivalent of an orchestra or a baseball team. You want to have some unexpected moments. You don't necessarily want to put the person who is a tremendous authority on eighteenth-century furniture as the designer for an eighteenth-century furniture exhibition. You choose somebody who has never really worked in that field before, but you have an instinctive feel that this person would work well with the material. You hope that he or she would reveal another dimension of the subject matter to the visitor of the exhibition.

> There are moments with certain exhibitions … that you hope will still resonate with people twenty years hence.

So, like the conductor of an orchestra, you have to make some creative connections yourself. You may decide – rather than have this person design the book, and that person design the catalog or the exhibition installation, and this curator do all the text labels and the storytelling – to bring somebody in as the grit in the oyster, somebody who is a natural fit, but not the most obvious fit.

The idea of an exhibition begins in the curator's mind. A curator may say, "I've always wanted to do an exhibition on such and such. It's a subject that has always fascinated me." And then he or she has to sell that idea to the museum's director and an exhibition committee often composed of trustees and external advisers. It is a bit like a newspaper reporter going to a paper's editor and saying, "I have a great story, I think we should run it," and trying to convince the editor that this is a good idea and a story worth running.

An exhibition needs drama. Deciding on an exhibition theme is a major event. In many ways, it is actually quite a crude medium for telling a very complicated story. We always look at many different options. We'll dismiss any ideas that we judge as having been done before or as not lending themselves very well to a visual analysis in a museum.

We have to ask ourselves: What are the objectives of this exhibition? What are the stories that we could tell with this exhibition? Is the theme a great idea or does it lend itself better for a book than an exhibition? You can't just walk through a museum gallery looking at photographs stuck on walls. That's a catalog or a wonderfully illustrated book. Neither can you treat it like a Public Broadcasting Service documentary – a story that may be too complex for an exhibition.

And then we have to face certain realities: What will be the cost? Are we certain that we can obtain the objects for it? Are we going to be able to borrow them? Can we afford to freight them from all the corners of the world?

And, most importantly: Who will be our target audience? Will there be enough people of all ages and all walks of life who will want to see such an exhibit? Or should we be targeting a specific audience? That is vital. If you think they're not likely to come, how are we going to fire their imagination to come and see an exhibition about something that they may know nothing about – a country, an era that they've never heard of? How do we connect with them and say, "Yes, you have never heard of this particular artist from this particular period, but this designer and his work could have incredible relevance to you today because …"

Or we may say, "We realize that this is a world far removed from your own, but let us start to capture your imagination. There may be relevance to some objects in this exhibit that will stimulate your imagination. Maybe we can actually start to try and get your dream process going."

So with an exhibition, we're not only working with creative people to develop the exhibition, we're trying to get to the DNA of the designer whose

Cooper-Hewitt Mansion on Fifth Avenue in New York.
Courtesy of Cooper-Hewitt

work we're showing and pull out those connective fields, so that they will entice people to come to the museum and see the exhibit. That's creative storytelling.

Our demographics actually switch quite distinctly depending on what kind of an exhibition we have. For example, an exhibition on fashion and color that we recently staged was the most successful show we've ever had here in terms of visitor numbers. It was huge because I think that a lot of people are very interested in fashion and are also interested in color. It was the merger of the two stories that attracted a lot of visitors.

In the main, our visitor is probably not hugely different from other museum visitors. They tend to be middle-class individuals, having a fairly high degree of educational background. And that's really what you would expect from a museum in this position.

For instance, I'm sure that people who came to our *Josef and Anni Albers: Design for Living* show were already pretty much familiar with the two Albers' work. They came because they were real fans of theirs. There were probably some young people who came because they wanted to explore that aesthetic but, in the main, the people who came to our show knew Anni's work in textile design from her show at the Jewish Museum a few years ago, and they knew that Josef was a painter, and they wanted to explore their work together.

Capturing the imagination in practical ways

The Cooper-Hewitt, National Design Museum was founded as a three-dimensional library, a resource for the designers and artisans of New York. The Hewitt sisters' idea was that this would elevate public taste and also

elevate design standards in the manufacturing industry and in the crafts generally. The sisters were looking for the beautiful and the everyday. That was their
mission. And in many ways, that ethos still stays with Cooper-Hewitt.

> There is very often a
> high degree of creativity
> in anything that is
> innovative, but I don't
> think it's a prerequisite.

We have a lot of scholars, but also a lot of practicing
designers, who come to the Cooper-Hewitt textile department, the wallpaper department, the drawings, prints and
design department seeking inspiration from works that we
have in our collection.

This brings up again the question: Do you have to be an
innovator to be creative? Personally, I don't believe you do. There is very often
a high degree of creativity in anything that is innovative, but I don't think it's a
prerequisite.

This became clear to me when a recent exhibition of sixteenth- and
seventeenth-century Ottoman caftans at the Smithsonian Museum in Washington so influenced the Belgian fashion designer Dries van Noten that he
based his whole collection last year on the inspiration that he drew from that
exhibition. So, how creative were these designs? How innovative were they?
Can you really draw a line between creativity and innovation?

Many designers come to the Cooper-Hewitt to go through our collection
with a similar sense of seeking inspiration. We have many students who sketch
in our galleries, trying to define their own visual style and their own sense of
creative identity from looking at the works of the past.

That is precisely what the Hewitt sisters had in mind when they set up the
museum. They wanted craftsmen and women – the artisans and the designers
of New York City – to be inspired by the examples from previous ages. The best
designs from the past were to inspire the future generations. We've always had
that sort of instructional and educative role at the museum.

There are many unusual opportunities for anyone interested in taking advantage of what the Cooper-Hewitt has to offer. For example, we probably have the
best lace collection in the world. If you were interested in lace, you would call
the museum and speak to the collections manager and identify the parameters
of what you are interested in seeing so that we would have some sense of what
you are looking for.

Based on that initial information, the collection manager would make an
appointment with you to come in and look at images, either on 35 mm slides or
in digital form, and seek more specific identification as to what sorts of pieces
would be of interest to you. Then we would physically pull them from our huge
collection that is based on site so that you could examine the real thing.

Obviously, with all this reference material being available here, we hope that the designers who come to us are not just plagiarizing something, just pulling something out from the collection and simply copying it. We hope that they're using it as an inspiration and then doing their own creations.

It's unfortunate when someone simply plagiarizes someone's work of art or design. Obviously the more you visit museums all over the world, the more likely you are to see historical precedent, and true originality, true creativity. The temptation of copying may be hard for some to resist.

There's nothing more unsatisfying than the sort of derivative, plagiarized, regurgitated piece of work that you look at and you think, "Well, I remember this the first time around." It is like pop music that *sounds* like the Beatles – it's that sort of sense.

There's a sort of gnawing sense of dissatisfaction looking, for example, at the chairs available these days and thinking, "You know, I can't think of anybody who has done anything as innovative with a chair since Charles and Ray Eames in the 1950s." They were endlessly exploring – whether it was with glass fiber or raw materials like teak, rosewood, walnut, and leather. Since then, nobody has managed to achieve that leap, that sense of creativity and real wholeness.

On the other hand, as you get a bit older and a bit more attuned to looking for creativity, you are occasionally drawn into confusing creativity with novelty. Just because something is novel doesn't mean that it's wildly creative or that it is wildly original. I mean, has Damien Hirst really done anything more to define art than Marcel Duchamp did before him?

Our brochure says, "Design is arguably the most accessible form of culture which impacts quality-of-life issues." This is how I want people to see our museum and our exhibits.

I want people to walk out of our museum and go down Fifth Avenue thinking about what they saw. And the further we can get them down Fifth Avenue still thinking about the subject, the more I believe that we've been successful.

I don't want our exhibits to be like people leaving a movie theater and, having just seen a pretty mediocre movie, forgetting it by the time they are back home. I don't want people to experience our art form in that way.

I want people to think, "You know, I'll never forget that show I saw at the Cooper-Hewitt. I must have been fifteen, but I can still remember the exhibition that they had there."

My singular goal is trying to get people to think more carefully about the process of design, how it has impacted their lives and what part it can play in their future.

MARVIN HAMLISCH

Composing and collaboration

Marvin Hamlisch's life in music is notable for its versatility. As a composer, he has won every major award: three Oscars, four Grammys, four Emmys, one Tony and three Golden Globe Awards. His groundbreaking show A Chorus Line *received a Pulitzer prize. He has composed many Broadway shows and more than forty motion picture scores, including his Oscar-winning score and song for* The Way We Were *and his adaptation of Scott Joplin's music for* The Sting. *He holds the position of Principal Pops Conductor with the Pittsburgh Symphony Orchestra as well as with the National Symphony Orchestra in Washington, DC.*

When you ask a great chef how much salt he puts in something, he will usually say, "Ah, you take a little handful here." It's the same with creative people. You can't quite quantify and you can't quite write directions on how to be creative. It's something that just happens because that is what creative people are all about.

I'll try to explain the creative process the best way I can. When you go to the UN and someone is speaking in a foreign language, they have people who simultaneously translate what they're hearing into your language, into English. So they're hearing something in one ear, and out of their mouth comes the translation in English.

In the same way, music is a language. The composer thinks about a song, thinks about what the song is trying to say, thinks about the kind of song he wants – if it's funny, if it's humorous, if it's dramatic, if it's love, if it's sad – and as he thinks about it in English, he simultaneously translates his thoughts into the musical language. Out of all that, a melody is born.

Creativity is a gift. If you harness it and if you give it its due, it can lead you to new vistas, new horizons, new ideas and new thoughts and it can be a very exciting ride. Most people who are "creative" just do it because they are imbued with it. For me, putting something on this earth that didn't exist yesterday is very fulfilling.

Marvin Hamlisch. *Photo: Shel Secunda*

Of course, creativity is not just in the province of show business people. I think most people have a creative streak in them, but not necessarily just in the arts. There are a lot of lawyers and accountants who can be very creative if they want to be. You can find a great teacher who can really motivate kids in school by creating very interesting assignments, and very stimulating classes. All these people can be very creative in their own right, even though they're not part of *show business*.

If you ask a dancer why they dance, they will say: "because I love dancing. I have to dance. I can do nothing else. I must dance." I think that's true of everybody in terms of creativity. You get this absolute, undeniable nudge from God and you have to do it. It's like breathing – you just do it to stay alive.

> ... that's true of everybody in terms of creativity. You get this absolute, undeniable nudge from God and you have to do it. It's like breathing – you just do it to stay alive.

Most creative people have a need for personal satisfaction. When you are creating, you create simply for the joy of it. When, all of a sudden, you receive an award for your work, it should be treasured, but not fought for. The intention should always be on writing something good, not on winning a race.

How I became a composer

My father was a musician and played six instruments. He came from Vienna and he was very creative. And my mother was a wonderful mother who could cook up a storm. I think that having the genes of my father was very helpful. I was able to start out pretty talented, and that was a very big gift to me.

My parents encouraged school and learning. I went to New York City's Professional Children's School, Queens College and Juilliard, all top-notch schools. This education was influential from the beginning toward my decision to get into the creative field.

I was very fortunate to have wonderful mentors. Jule Styne, the composer, was very helpful, compassionate and considerate. You need someone who takes you under his wing and gives you a boost, and he was very much like that. He was a wonderful and giving human being. I was an assistant vocal arranger on a few of his shows, and he let me see how he created – how he did it. It was a very exciting process.

As I grew up, they were many composers I especially admired. The person whose legend I admire the most is Leonard Bernstein. He certainly has inspired me, especially after hearing his *West Side Story*.

How I like to work

New ideas for music depend on a number of circumstances. For example, if you're writing about 1830s Vienna, you're going to write differently from writing about New York City in 2007. So the actual locale and time of a certain situation has a lot to do with how you're going to write. You let the situations, characters, and the events inspire you.

When I write songs, the first thing I do is think about the kind of song I want to write, just in terms of the *feel*. Not about anything else except the *feel*. If there is a title, either in my head or in the lyricist's head, I try first, at the piano, to find the *feel* – not even a melody so much, just the rhythm – the thing that somehow or other is going to steer this song into a direction. Then I start looking for melodies. Sometimes these come very quickly, sometimes they take forever, and sometimes they never come.

There are times when writing a song comes easy. But, other times, there can be sequences that you try to write, and nothing evolves. When I run into such a roadblock, the best thing for me to do is just stop. I wait until the next day and hope that inspiration will come.

That's the process. Sometimes you get very lucky and you write something very quickly. More often, it takes a lot of time.

I love writing Broadway musicals because they are collaborative efforts. I'm not like a painter who can just wake up in the morning, go to the park and paint. I don't work that way. I tend to need other people around me as collaborators and to also come up with good ideas – an idea for a book, a story – all these things. I need other people to create along with me.

> ... collaboration is a very important part of my work.

If you find the right people and they have the right ideas, you're off and running. That's why collaboration is a very important part of my work. Of course, you try to find people who are on the same wavelength and want to do what *you* want to do.

That's show biz

With *A Chorus Line*, everything came from the story idea. A very slow, meticulous, two steps forward, one step back process in which there were a lot of ideas in the ethos. And slowly but surely you started to differentiate between these ideas, and you started to say, "Ah, this is a good one," or, "No, that doesn't make it," or "This could work," or "This could not work."

The creators were not thinking about how commercial the show would be,

A Chorus Line won nine Tony Awards in 1976 including "Best Musical Score." In 1990 it became the longest running show in Broadway history, and has toured worldwide successfully.
Photo: Richard Gerstman

and we weren't thinking about how long it would run. We just were thinking, "Let's do something different, and make it as good as we can."

My other activities

When I'm not working, I love to travel. I love the South of France. I love Tuscany. I love Prague. And I'm also definitely a big fan of the Napa Valley. I tend to go to these places to recharge the batteries. To me, vacations are a vital pause from the work mode.

And then there is the need for educating young people. I believe that we need much more music involvement in schools. We need to start to get the arts to be up on the platform where they should be. This is not a little happy-go-lucky option for one's life. It should be an absolute necessity, and it is shameful that it's not in every school.

I try to do anything I can to light a fire under the world of the arts. I give speeches about it. I talk to kids about it. I sometimes come into schools and lecture. When a community can have money for a soccer field, there's no reason that they can't also have an arts program. It doesn't have to be one or the other.

As for my future plans, I hope to get another show on Broadway.

Let's face it, that's *What I Do For Love*.

STEVEN HOLL

Breaking the rules

Steven Holl was named "America's Best Architect" in 2001 by Time *magazine. His architectural achievements range from museums to chapels, to embassies, to academic and residential projects in the United States, as well as in the Netherlands, France, Belgium, Austria and China. The Kiasma, Museum of Contemporary Art in Helsinki, Finland, is considered his masterpiece, as is the expansion of the Nelson-Atkins Museum of Art in Kansas City, Missouri. His numerous prestigious awards include France's Grande Médialle d'Or, Finland's Alvar Aalto Medal, and the National Design Award of Architecture from Cooper-Hewitt, National Design Museum.*

How do you define creativity?

I think that creativity is breaking out of the habitual ways of thinking, approaching anything you are doing in a creative way. Breaking out of habitual patterns that often times are not the best ways of doing things.

I feel that what we need in the world right now is a big dose of creativity on a whole national planning level. As an architect, I am not just talking about buildings. I am talking about how to preserve the natural landscapes and how to live our lives. This model of suburban big box stores, subdivisions, sprawl, and dependence on petroleum to get us from point A to point B – this is uncreative. These are habitual ways of thinking and it is time that we realized that we need to change this.

We need a new program to unlearn all these habitual ways and have new and creative ways to think about how we're going to occupy the earth. Creativity is not just for artistic entertainment. Creativity is central to our survival. Imagination is central to our survival. Without these, we are dead.

From early tinkering to professionalism

I grew up together with my brother James, who is a sculptor and an artist, in Bremerton, Washington. It's a no man's land, a military town. There were only about 30,000 people living in Bremerton at the time. It was a typical American

Steven Holl at his desk surrounded by his sketchbooks from many years. *Photo: Richard Gerstman*

town with the main street, and J.C. Penney's and Oldberg's Drugstore. The only thing that made Bremerton unique was the Puget Sound Naval Shipyard where they built aircraft carriers.

Creativity is not just for artistic entertainment. Creativity is central to our survival.

They had this thing called the "Hammerhead Crane," which is like a four-story building hanging on the back of a crane. It would pick up the superstructures of aircraft carriers and pieces of submarines. As a kid, seeing this kind of activity going on was visually totally fascinating.

When I try to remember all this in terms of my current activities, this is probably where it all got started. There was no architecture in Bremerton, but there was all this amazing work going on – different kinds of things being built in this shipyard.

Very early in my life, when I was about five or six years old, my brother and I played a game that we called "property." We built things and we were kind of competing against each other with what we were building. We started this very early in the day, sometimes between five and seven in the morning. I can remember being outside working for maybe two hours, when our mother would call us for breakfast.

We would build small "villages" in the backyard and make cars move around the "buildings." At one time, we built a three-story tree house with a cabana on the ground, and an underground "clubhouse." We dug a big hole, then used logs and old rugs and piled dirt on them to make a roof, so you could get down inside our "clubhouse." That was our secret hideout to play with fire and stuff like that.

My father has just turned eighty-six. He was always very creative and he still draws very well. He lives in Manchester, Washington, and every time I go out there, we have a drawing contest. I draw him and he draws me in different ways. We call it the Manchester sketchbook.

My father was inherently artistic, and he made things by hand. Imagination was something that he loved. He would make different things himself. He even built part of the first house that I designed in Manchester, Washington. This was when I graduated from the University of Washington School of Architecture, in 1972. The house was finished in 1974.

My parents still live in that first house that I drew. I drew this house so that it was all vertical on two squares, and it had a staircase that was curved and connected three levels. The contractor looked at the plans and said, "Well, I can build the house, but I can't build that staircase." So my father said, "Well, I'll build the staircase myself." And he went so fast that the stairs were coming up out of the ground like a little skyscraper while the rest of the house hadn't reached as high as the stairs yet. My father was way ahead of the contractor.

My parents, both mom and dad, were both incredibly encouraging. They encouraged my brother to go ahead and pursue a career in art and encouraged me to pursue architecture. At one point my mother said, "Don't you think you want to be a naval architect and get a sure job in the shipyard here in Bremerton?" I said, "No way. That's being an engineer, planning to build the big ships – military ships. I want to get out of Bremerton and be an architect."

We're a very prolific family. My wife is also an artist. She does unique work using video cameras. My brother is a tenured professor at Marymount College in New York. He has a collection of great paintings and sculptures that he makes and he shows. And his wife is a photographer. So, in my family, all of us speak the same appreciative language of real imaginative thought.

Thinking beyond the habitual mode

A creative person has to have imagination instead of thinking of everything as being comfortably acceptable. Even in the sciences you find that the subjective has to be merged with the objective. You cannot find out anything about things that you don't know if you just think in a pragmatic, objective way. You have to let the dream occur – you have to have a dream intersecting. So it's critical that the subjective has to penetrate the objective thinking. You'll never find another way if you keep going down the same old path.

> A creative person has to have imagination instead of thinking of everything as being comfortably acceptable.

Just think of people like James Watson and Francis Crick. They figured out the secret of life, the structure of DNA, the double helix. They didn't find it plodding along in a straight line. One of them had a dream one night of a snake swallowing its tail, and came to the studio the next day and sketched the double helix – and there was the brilliant creative work of biology and genetics. That did not come from a pragmatic approach. It came from an inspirational moment, a dream.

That is similar to how I always try to get into my architectural projects. Getting through the whole process can be difficult, but moving from conception to when you see a project completed is a very fulfilling thrill. That's the excitement and fulfillment of doing creative work.

> You cannot find out anything about things that you don't know if you just think in a pragmatic, objective way.

The way I work is to start every day in the morning and paint for one hour. For years I've used the same 5 × 7-in. British-made watercolor pads to do little paintings or drawings, and I have every drawing that

I've done for the last twenty-five years. It has become a kind of second memory bank for me.

Sometimes I sketch a building. Or I may think about something that I haven't done before. I don't have any constraints. Sometimes I just get up and drift and let the imagination have a free rein. Other times I think about an actual project.

It's a technique that kind of loosens me up. A lot of times, my architectural creations start with these early sketches.

Sometimes it's just a painting – just drifting – and sometimes my sketches are not even good. They may be just throwaways. One of the things about creativity is that you can't do everything well all the time. Some mornings I may be hung over or I don't feel good and I do crummy drawings. Another day, I may be looking at something by Matisse, the great colorist, and that gives me inspiration.

I have a shelf over my drawing board full of my drawing pads. These little books in my archive are a kind of history of my architectural fantasies. In one of these books you can find the first sketch for the big dormitory we did at MIT.

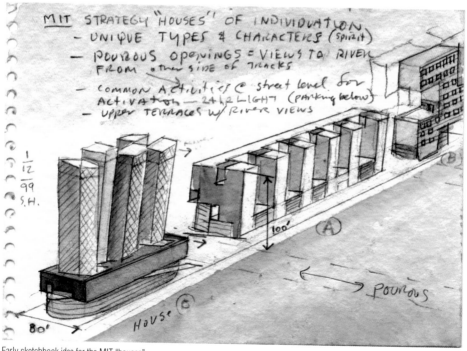

Early sketchbook idea for the MIT "houses".
Courtesy of Steven Holl Architects

I go through two or more of these every month. So with twenty-four or twenty-eight pads per year and twenty-five years of doing this, there's lot of material. It's a kind of catalog of my first creative impulses and I can trace back these first impulses very easily.

Other times, I have to work with severe time restraints, such as doing a project in less than a month.

Early sketchbook idea for Beijing, China project.
Courtesy of Steven Holl Architects

This includes the floor plans, all the sections and all the mechanical drawings. In short, how the whole thing works. I have the help of four people on my staff who are really good and work very hard. But my ideas often start with that early morning sketch – the first creative impulse – and we go on from there.

The key is study and intuition

The key to solving an architectural problem is to know the problem well. You have studied all the aspects. You know the basic needs. And then you wake up in the morning and start to work. All the time, you have to keep this intuition in your mind, allowing it to penetrate into the pragmatics. It's very key that the intuition can penetrate to the pragmatics and that they work together. Then you have a creative solution.

> Successful creative people have to be very persuasive

If you try to do it with intuition alone, it becomes just a mess. If you just try to do it with the pragmatics alone, just the facts, that doesn't lead anywhere either. That is, unfortunately, how a lot of buildings are done and why they are so raw and nasty. They don't have any energy, or passion, or any inspiration in them. But it's hard to get the developers to agree to allow inspiration to happen. They just want to get it done fast and easy.

Successful creative people have to be very persuasive, because in order to become successful with your creations, you sometimes have to try and persuade people who cannot be persuaded very easily.

I'm not that persuasive. What motivates me is that I love to see the spaces and to have the thrill of taking an original idea to a certain level of execution –

getting it built and being able to walk inside it. There is so much energy in that, so that it's hard to explain.

If I were a composer and I spent three years writing a symphony and finally had someone pull together the orchestra and play that symphony for the first time – it would be my thrill. That's the energy given back to a creative person.

The great thing about architecture is that year after year it gives back to people who go into the building. Take the museum we did in Helsinki – I still get messages from people saying how great they think it is and how they love the spaces when they go through that museum.

The building is right in the center of Helsinki. So I imagined taking certain slices in the building and allowing visitors to look out and see the Parliament building, and see the adjacent city at key moments during the sequence of the slices throughout the

> What motivates me is that I love to see the spaces and to have the thrill of taking an original idea to a certain level of execution

galleries. The resulting plays of light, the view from the museum and how that building connects to the city through just these little slices was even more successful than I had hoped for.

Whenever you do a project overseas, you need to remember that you are in a different country at a different locale, with a different client, a different atmosphere, different materials, and different ways of understanding space. And that has to affect your thinking.

In Beijing, we're doing a big project. It's near the Forbidden City and you can see into the Forbidden City from it. It's a series of eight buildings that are connected by bridges.

One of the things about working in Beijing is that there is a real belief in feng shui, which means not using beams because to the Chinese being underneath a beam brings bad luck. Therefore, we decided that there would be no beams. Instead, we brought the structure to the outside. Floors span to the core of the buildings and by using flat plates from the core to the outside of the buildings we need no beams.

Then there is also the notion of Chinese polychroming. We took the *I Ching* and Tibetan Buddhist temple colors and colored the underside of the bridges and the soffits in the building. So the colors throughout the buildings are derived from Chinese polychroming.

Left: Simmons Hall, MIT, Cambridge, Massachusetts, USA.
Photo: Paul Warchol

Breaking the rules

In architecture, from the beginning of having an inspiration – an original idea – and working through all the constraints can take years.

As an example of my way of handling such a project creatively, let me take you into a major project of ours: the Nelson-Atkins Museum in Kansas City. It's a great, great art museum that has a collection comparable to the Metropolitan Museum of Art in New York.

The project started as a competition between six architects who were selected from twenty candidates originally considered by the museum.

The project involved the expansion of the Nelson-Atkins Museum, a 1937 building. The six competing architects, including ourselves, were given the rules that we could not change the front of the museum and that the only location for the expansion of the museum should be at the back of the building.

All the other five architects followed these rules and put the expansion in back of the building, as requested.

To me, that meant blocking the north façade, blocking the entry to the museum and disregarding the landscape around the museum. So I broke the rules.

When I met with the museum directors, I questioned the rules and then I brought up the subjective – the idea of fusing architecture and landscape. I felt that you didn't need to just build the building as an object. I wanted to bring everything together, relating to each other.

I said to the board of directors, "You should make this expansion project part of the landscape, keeping the north side of the building free and making a grand arrival court with a big reflecting pond."

We won the assignment because the jury had the energy and the belief that our scheme's idea was a positive direction. It took eight years from the time we started to complete the construction of the site. This is a long time, but it was really an exciting project.

But in a museum, different dimensions come into play, such as those needed for the systems of air conditioning and humidification, because it's very important that no harm is done to the artwork. Right in the first sketch I suggested using a "breathing T system" that would bring light down to the galleries and connect that light to the workings of the HVAC (heating, ventilation and air conditioning) system.

The breathing Ts are T-shaped structural elements that are covered with translucent, insulated glass planks and the HVAC system comes inside them. That way you solve the light problem and, at the same time, you can bring air from around and above. And as we began to develop different things, I decided that you could actually mix the south light and the north light and get a kind of modulation of the quality of light – cool light and warm light through this breathing T system.

These types of projects need a lot of pragmatic work. The creativity part in the beginning is crucial to get it going in the right direction. After that, good pragmatics represent 95 percent of the project. But if you don't have the 5 percent creative part in the beginning, the 95 percent of pragmatics can just be for a big ugly box that's depressing. It may work perfectly, but it's not inspirational and it's not great architecture – it's just a big piece of space that does its job.

And what is the job of architecture if it isn't to inspire? What is the job of a museum if it isn't to excite, to inspire and to determine how the body moves through the spaces? If you cut out that 5 percent of creativity in the beginning and just go to the box solution, you really cut out the heartbeat and all you get is the body and the skeleton.

It's like the human body. There's the soul and then there are all the other body parts – the lungs and the liver and all the other organs – needed to make the body work. But if you don't have the soul, it is just a dead body walking. So, you could say that even if the creative part may be only a 5 percent piece of architecture while 95 percent is sweat and engineering, it's the 5 percent that gets everything going in the right direction.

It's like a 150-car freight train running down a track, and there is one ten-year-old kid who can switch the track to make the train go this way or that way. Even though the freight train has incredible horsepower and tons of force, this ten-year-old kid can throw the switch. That switch represents the 5 percent creativity part. Throw the switch one way and that freight train will go down in one direction. Throw the switch the other way and the train will go a completely different way. One of the ways can be full of energy and excitement, the other can be boring and negative and just depressing.

To control it, I need to be at the switch. I need to be that ten-year-old who controls that switch. The responsibility of the architect is to have control of that switch so that everything goes in the right direction.

Controlling the direction

Some architects will worry too much about how a building problem is going to be solved before they worry about how it's going to be created.

To me, two things have to happen in the beginning of every project. First, there is the competition and I am doing the conceptualizing. Secondly, I am breaking the rules. I am insisting that the way that a project must be approached is not to rely on habitual ways of thinking about it. If necessary, I will say, "No, take a different route. Find a creative solution first and solve the pragmatic problems later."

You can't do this without being willing to force the possibility of moving your client out of the habitual way of thinking into another way of thinking, and letting the subjective come into the process. After that, you can turn to solving the practical issues.

There's a great story about Jorn Utzon, the Danish architect of the Sydney Opera House. He had this inspiration of creating the Sydney Opera House as if it were reflecting the sails in the harbor. It's the first great piece of twentieth-century iconic architecture and it put the city on the map. Before that, Sydney was relatively unknown around the world. That building is now on their stamps and on their money – it has made Sydney a destination city. That's the result of a creative impulse.

Utzon had a great patron client in the prime minister at that time. But when the prime minister died, someone else came into office – a very republican, conservative and rural guy – who campaigned that this architect was extravagant and wasting the city's money. He cut off the fees, so Utzon left and went back to Denmark. Some "meat and potatoes" architects got in there to finish it. So the building has never been what it could have been on the inside.

But recently, Utzon, now 87 years old, has been invited back to rebuild the interiors according to his ideas. His sons are acting on his behalf, but he's calling the shots from his home in Denmark. So, even fifty years later, they realized in Sydney that when they took away the creative part of the equation, they lost something essential. This is an example of what can happen when you switch tracks away from a creative intuition.

> Find a creative solution first and solve the pragmatic problems later.

Architecture is always a balancing act. You have to give and take. You may be a fantastically gifted architect, but you soon realize that to do great architecture it also takes a great client. It's never just the architect.

This applies even when doing a small house. I recently finished a house in Phoenix, Arizona, called the Planer House. It's a tilt up concrete structure with light coming down – a very beautiful house. It was possible only because the client wanted something special. It would never have happened without a great client.

Defining success

Success in any creative endeavor is very hard to measure. So, how do you measure success in creative terms?

When we speak about architecture, realizing success is very rare. It isn't very often that we can consummate something as creative as the Guggenheim Museum in New York. It took many years to realize it, but that building is an incredibly ambitious spatial work. This was Frank Lloyd Wright's great success, even if it's not seen as a success in everybody's eyes.

Is money a measure of success? I think not. I would never measure success in terms of money. I know some really wealthy people that I don't consider successful.

Is success having a large office with a lot of people? People sometimes ask me how many people work in my office. Who cares? Le Courbusier, at the end of his life, had five people in his office. Louis Kahn's office, the year before he died, had more work than he had ever had in his life and he had just sixteen people. So, how many people work in the office is not a measure of success.

So what then defines creative success?

I have lot of dreams. I measure my success by my ability to realize an architectural dream that comes as close as possible to my vision and my hope of finalizing a creative project. I see this as an offering that a lot of other people can enjoy.

I'm very much an architect who likes to do socially open works – works that can be more of a contribution to the public than to just private ownership. I'm always dedicating myself more towards public works. The work for the Pratt School of Architecture, a glass-enclosed bridge between two older buildings that provides several levels of working space, is very valuable in my mind as a creative success, even though I made the first drawings in 1997 and it took all these years to realize it.

Is winning awards success? I've won some awards and I appreciate them, but I think that most awards are just posturing by some organization trying to be important. For example, I participate in the AIA (American Institute of Architects) awards. AIA is the official organization representing and promoting architects. My firm has won several awards there. But I fear that there is often a tendency to be self-congratulatory whether or not it is deserved.

There are architecture firms that identify themselves as "an award winning architecture firm." It's really boring, this award system. It's all about publicity and hype and manipulation, instead of great creativity.

Chapel of St. Ignatius, Seattle University, Seattle, Washington, USA. *Photo: Paul Warchol*

To my mind, awards are not a true measure of success. But to keep alive as an architect, to get another project, you have to be able to say that you won an AIA award. It's a rat race that doesn't have anything to do with a careful assessment by really good minds of the quality of what you can do. I cherish most a critique by people whom I respect, who have done some creative work themselves. That is much more valuable to me than any award.

Some time ago, I did the St. Ignatius Chapel on the campus of Seattle University of which I'm very proud. It was my first building close to my old hometown of Bremerton – Seattle is across the bay. And it won an AIA award.

But then, something happened that was really meaningful to me.

One day, I was in a supermarket there and when I paid my bill with my credit card, which says architect on it, the checkout lady said, "Oh, you're an architect. You should go and see this chapel at Seattle University. That's a piece of architecture." She didn't know that I was the architect of that chapel. But that checkout lady in the supermarket recognized that chapel as a great piece of architecture – and that, to me, was much more meaningful and much more rewarding than any award.

> If what you do is creatively stimulating and exciting and inspirational to those who experience it – that, for me, will always be a true measure of my success.

Whatever it was that communicated to her, it was not something abstract or arcane or hard to understand or that had an experiential dimension. That, I think, is the test. If it's really a creative work of architecture, anybody has to be able to understand it. If you can walk into it, see the light and see the space – that is success.

If what you do is creatively stimulating and exciting and inspirational to those who experience it – that, for me, will always be a true measure of my success.

ILANA GOOR

My best things are my mistakes

Ilana Goor's sculptures are uncompromisingly spontaneous and inspiring. Born in Tiberias, Israel, she has lived in New York City most of her life, but her ties to her native country are strong. She opened a museum in Jaffa, Israel, that has become a major tourist attraction. Never having studied art formally, her creative output covers a vast landscape, including sculptures, decorative belt buckles, elaborately decorated gold jewelry and furniture and accessories utilizing uncommonly used iron "rebar." Her works have been exhibited in Italy, France, Switzerland, Germany and the United States. One of her most emotionally moving works is a large bronze sculpture at Yad Vashem, the Holocaust memorial museum in Jerusalem.

I don't know about creativity. I just know that I always wanted to be an artist. I don't think that you become an artist – I believe that you are *born* an artist.

I come from a family of five generations of doctors. My mother was a doctor. She liked to draw a lot when she was home and not working in the hospital. At that time, we lived in Israel in a Bauhaus-style house, so that I grew up in an environment of good taste right from the beginning.

Dyslexia and creativity

As a kid, and all my life as far back as I can remember, I was always by myself. I suffered from dyslexia and, at that time, nobody knew anything about dyslexia. I was kicked out of every school. In first grade and second grade, when I was six or seven years old, people said to my mother, "Something is wrong with your daughter. She's not focused. In the middle of the class she walks outside. We have no control over her. Move her on to another school. She'd be better off there – but not in our school."

My mother didn't know what dyslexia was, even though she was a doctor. But she would say to them, "Leave my daughter alone, she's a genius." So I never really "suffered" from the dyslexia. I saw what I saw, I did what I did, and I never had parents who would say, "Go do your homework. Why are you not as good

Ilana Goor. *Courtesy of Ilana Goor*

in this or that like other children?" My parents never compared me to anybody. And that saved me.

My father was in the British army. He was in Egypt and in Persia – now called Iran – and so he was not home much. My mother was always working and so she was not home much either. She didn't know about cooking – she had a cook and a maid who took us to school. Twice a year, my mother went to Switzerland to buy shoes, since she was crazy about shoes. But whenever she was home, she always gave me confidence so that for me the sky is the limit.

... every creation is like a new birth

I never had any schooling. I learned everything from the street. Yes, the street. Most of my friends in various fields are people who have much more knowledge than I have. I don't read. I know how to read, but I don't read. I have to learn everything by listening. You tell me something and I understand it much more than if I would read about it. Because the minute I finish reading something I forget it. But if you impress me with what you're telling me, I'll learn everything about it, because I'm interested.

I am like a child who can play the piano even though the child never had any piano lessons. And wouldn't it be nice if we could stay being children forever? We may have a little wrinkle, or a little pain, or some broken bones – but, in some ways, creative people always remain children.

I firmly believe that creative people live longer than other people. Why? Because every creation is like a new birth, new excitement, new stimulation and preparing for the next creative venture.

I don't know whether my dyslexia has anything to do with my creativity. Quite a few dyslectic people are creative. Churchill was dyslectic. Picasso was dyslectic. But I also know some dyslectic people who are actually crippled – they cannot do anything.

But me, dyslexia or not, I've always been creative. I've never known any other life.

Seeing more than anyone else

I always felt that I could look at things and I could see much more than anyone else. It's very hard for me to explain. For example, when I was very young and didn't have a lot of money, I would go shopping with several people and come out of the stores with fabulous things that they never even saw.

I always loved to create things. As a kid, I was always busy making my own toys. Now, my house in New York City is very, very, eclectic. I have modern, I have old, and I have antique things. I buy things not by knowledge, but by feeling. I'm the one who designed the setting and so everything fits. If another creative person were involved, it would be his or her taste. But this has been created by one person – me – and so the arrangement and the colors all fit.

Maybe this is because, for me, home is the most important thing in life. I always felt that that's the place where you should spend most of your time and, therefore, you want it to be beautiful.

Because my head is so full of ideas and creating things, I have to get up in the morning in a perfect house. Often, when you walk into an artist's studio, it's the biggest mess. Sometimes, you can't even see the artwork that's supposed to be there. But with me, because my surroundings are so mixed up in my head, everything in the house has to be very organized, very neat, and suited to my taste.

My taste and my creativity are rooted in my past. People in Israel sometimes say to me, "How long have you been in the United States?" I say, "All my life." I came to the United States very young and have lived here for forty-eight years. And all this time, while I love the United States, I have remained the same Israeli that I always was. You can never get away from the roots that you acquired in the early years of your life.

People try very hard to get away from their roots – but the truth is that you can never get away from them. The Russians who come to New York – they all live in the same area and they all speak Russian, because it's familiar to them. You can go to Chinatown and it's all Chinese. You can go to Little Italy and it's all Italian. It's very, very difficult for the first generation to discard their roots.

Being a creative person, I believe that my roots are the most important things in my life. You should respect your roots, because without your roots you will never grow creatively.

> You should respect your roots, because without your roots you will never grow creatively.

I do all sorts of art. For me, art is anything that I like. To some people, some of my work is grotesque. I say, "What can it do to you? Why should you be afraid of it?" I'm not afraid to live with new and different ideas.

A recent article in *Haaretz*, the most prominent magazine in Israel, said that I'm searching for something that does not exist. True. But that's the way I work. I get up in the morning, I open the door, and my mind starts working. And that often leads to unexpected happy accidents.

Unexpected happy accidents

Let me give you a small example of how this happens: I love making things for myself to wear. At one point, my husband, Lenny, was looking for a certain kind of a belt but didn't find anything in the stores that he liked. So, I made one or two belts for him.

One day, when Lenny and I were walking around Bloomingdale's, a young fellow in his late twenties or early thirties came over to us and said, "I love that buckle and belt. Where did you buy it?" So my husband said, "My wife made it." And the man said, "Well, I'm a buyer for Bloomingdale's. Could she make some more for Bloomingdale's? I need a collection, at least seven different designs." So I said, "Okay, I'll be back with something in a week" and I flew to Israel that very night.

That was the beginning of a $2,000,000 belt design business. Eventually, the belts were sold everywhere, at Neiman Marcus, Saks Fifth Avenue – in about 1,800 department stores.

And what happened to the belts? After three years of being the best-selling belts, people started copying them for the cheap shops on Broadway – not Saks Fifth Avenue. It's difficult to copyright design. All you have to do is change the original a little. You can be the most creative individual but, unfortunately, you cannot copyright creativity.

It was a good experience anyway, because it gave me quite a bit of self-confidence. I felt, at that time, that making money was the gate to freedom. I felt that I could create whatever came to my mind and it would sell.

Another happy accident was in the winter of 1984, around the time when I started designing my furniture. I walked outside the door on a day when there was very high snow and I saw a broken sled that someone had left on a pile of garbage.

I took it and drove to my iron works in Brooklyn and started designing a rocking chair, which was somewhat reminiscent of the old sled.

Originally we had a problem with it because nobody wanted to buy it. And I loved that chair. Why? Because for me it seemed to float. But it was very, very long and, in a small apartment in New York, people were afraid to stumble over the chair. One day Lenny

Ilana Goor's Rocking Chair won the Roseo Award in 1988 for residential seating.
Courtesy of Ilana Goor

said, "Ilana, you have to cut it and make it shorter." I said, "Cut it? No way. I'm not cutting it." For Lenny, who is a businessman, selling is everything. But for me, an artist – I'm not going to change my ideas for anybody or anything. Eventually, the chair became the biggest success and the best item that we had.

Making my home a museum

At about the same time, I opened my home in Jaffa, Israel, to the public by turning it into a museum. I added a little gift shop in my museum. Initially, I showed things by different craftspeople from Israel to help those who had trouble selling what they made. And people in Israel were very excited about it because, previously, people who came to my museum would never look at work by another artist. They only wanted a souvenir from Ilana Goor.

The museum is now one of the main attractions in Tel Aviv and Jaffa. Over a million people have visited the museum and there I met many interesting people, like Bill Clinton, fashion designer Donna Karan, and Ralph Lauren – people whom I would never have met otherwise.

But most people who come to Israel for an occasional visit don't know me. They only come because they've heard of the museum or read somewhere about it. I know that most of these people could not afford to buy my bronze sculptures. So we decided to start making aluminum dishes. All the dishes had decorations representing birds. I don't really like birds and I would prefer the dishes to be very clean. But people like little ornaments and so I added the birds. We also made forks and knives, also with little birds.

I make these commercial things only for the gift shop. An artist must sell to stay alive, if not for her own ego. Because if you sit with your own art forever and nothing is happening, you get depressed and you become bitter. And when you are depressed and bitter, it's very difficult to work. Work has to be a pleasure.

Usually, I work with different types of materials. I love to collect all kinds of old things. I put them together and call them hybrids.

At first, I couldn't sell my artwork. I kept motivated by doing things for myself and I never did anything just to please anybody. This actually turned out to be my good luck, because it led to my designing furniture that again became a multi-million dollar business.

Like the belts, my furniture design also started by complete coincidence. In Israel, one night, Yitzak Rabin, the Israeli prime minister at the time, asked me if I could accommodate something like thirty-five people on the roof of my new house in Jaffa. I agreed, but since I had just finished building the house, I didn't have any tables. In fact, I didn't have anything.

But I found some material that had been left on the roof of the house by the contractor. This material, called rebar, is put into the cement in order to strengthen the cement. Usually, you see this material thrown into the street while the construction of a building is going on. It's rusty material and nobody had ever used rebar before for anything else.

I took it to make a plain table out of it, using the rebar for the table legs. Then I went to a glass place where they showed me some thick, bulletproof glass that was left over from the 1948 war. The glass was badly scratched but I took all they had and made about seven tables – each measuring one meter by one meter.

Later, I added some birds, not as part of the table structure but just to sit on the glass as decoration. The tables became a big seller because of the birds. People think that I'm a bird lady, but I actually can't stand birds. How can you love birds when they give no love in return?

When I did the tables, I hadn't anticipated doing something extraordinary. But then, using rebar, I also made some lamps, some other tables and a chair, and took them to Art Expo. My husband was not really convinced that doing this was worthwhile.

> If you want to be creative, you have to develop your own signature.

But in America, anything is possible. Just think of Andy Warhol who took Brillo packages and Campbell's soup cans and made paintings with them. Or Marcel Duchamp who used an old toilet and made a piece of artwork out of it. It shows you that anything is possible.

I didn't realize that by using this rebar – a readymade building material that's rusty and unattractive and that nobody uses except for construction – I could create artwork. And the material is very, very difficult for me to use because it controls you – you don't control the material.

But Andy Warhol came to my show and he said to me, "Ilana, you're going to make millions of dollars." And I said, "Why?" He said, "Because you're the first one who used the rebar material creatively." That weekend, Lenny sold about $150,000 worth of tables.

After that, Lenny and I decided to take space in the D&D – Designers & Decorators – building in New York City, because that's where the architects come to look for things. Lenny sold the belt company and, in a matter of one year, I had twenty-two showrooms in the United States for my furniture.

Feeling good

I have a lot of self-confidence. At an early age, you get the confidence from your parents. They can instill confidence in you or they can ruin you. I was lucky that I got confidence, so that I always feel that whatever I want to do, I can do.

Ilana Goor's *Woman Against The Wind* bronze statue in Tel Aviv.
Courtesy of Ilana Goor

I don't know whether my self-confidence is the reason why I have a talent, but I create with confidence. I never had a teacher and never wanted a teacher. Because, when you're a student, you always want to be like your teacher. I can see it from my students. They do everything they see in a book. If you want to be creative, you have to develop your own signature.

I like to do anything that I feel like doing this minute. I feel that I have reached a point where I can get up in the morning, and decide what I want to do that particular day. I'm doing clothes now and jewelry and I have a wonderful leather line. Donna Karan, the well-known fashion designer, visited my museum in Jaffa when she was in Israel and loved my designs so much that she bought some clothes and some of my furniture.

Early in my career, when my husband and I were living in California, I wanted to have a studio. Everybody in California who did anything had to have a studio. I never had a studio before. When I said to Lenny, "I would like to have a little studio that I could play in," he said, "Who do you think you are – Rodin?"

Then I realized that if you really have it in you, you don't need a studio. When I have an idea, I go to my workroom or to a metal shop, and I work there without a precise plan. I don't measure. I never learned how to measure anything. I pick up the material and start working. Everything is by the eye. I really do my work in a primitive way.

But it's very difficult for me to plan anything in advance. I do make tables that I want to sell and I add the animals, like a little frog or some birds. But this is not really creative and, therefore, it's not exciting for me.

As for me, I always just wanted to be myself. The director of the Guggenheim once said to me, "The good thing about you is that you really don't know the rules."

The Holocaust statue

I had my first show in 1976 when Bill McCann, who was the director of the County Museum in Los Angeles, saw some of the work that I had done – a painted trunk, chairs and sculptures made out of clay.

He asked me, "Who did all those?" And when I said, "I did," he said, "Would you like to have a show at the County Museum?" I was stunned – I couldn't believe it. But he said, "You really have something in you that is very interesting." That's how it all started.

At that point I began to realize that maybe I really did have something. Then, one day, the ambassador for Israel in Los Angeles called me and said, "Ilana, there will be a show in Los Angeles to celebrate twenty-five years of Jerusalem. Would you like to participate?" I said, "With what?" He said, "To make a statue representing the Holocaust."

To tell you the truth, I really didn't know that much about the Holocaust. I knew that six million Jews had been killed, but none of my family was among them – or, at least, my family never talked about it at home. But I decided to do it. I went to Israel to visit Yad Vashem, the Holocaust memorial museum in Jerusalem, and another Holocaust museum near Nahariya, to get the feeling of what to do.

I decided right away that I did not want another dead person hanging on an electric fence. I wanted something different. I had no instructions what height the piece should be or what weight. I didn't know anything. I was working in my garage because I didn't even have a studio to work in. But I decided to have a huge woman with big shoulders, carrying a dead child with shoes in its feet. Why the shoes? When you die with bare feet, you are in a hospital, but when people die with their shoes on, they're not ready for it. So I made the child wearing shoes, and the woman walking very proudly, not showing any suffering. Her head is faceless, resembling the exhaust of an oven at a concentration camp where they incarcerated the bodies of the people they had gassed.

Teddy Kollek, then the mayor of Jerusalem, came to the exhibition to open it, and was so moved by the sculpture that he sent a committee from Yad Vashem who asked me to cast the statue in bronze. It is now standing in Yad Vashem.

So, things just happen. I don't plan. I don't want to please – I'm the way I am. For me, every new work is the exciting work. But once I complete it, it's finished.

I love working with different readymade materials, like the rebar I used for the tables and the chairs. The material is often stronger than you, and it takes years of working with the material to conquer it.

That's what was so great about Henry Moore. He had the guts to use various materials and take advantage of their characteristics. Most sculptors are afraid of using material with which they are not familiar. So they use the same material all the time, and they rub it and shine it instead of taking advantage of it. Moore was the first one who was not afraid of cutting through it and using it differently.

When things don't fit

I consider myself very lucky because I love to work. I don't know any other life. I enjoy every moment of my life. Every time I do something that I like, it makes me very happy, if only for a minute.

Occasionally, I've done some projects that have made me unhappy, where I got to a point and said, "I don't like it and I'm going to abandon this" and I walked away from it.

For instance, I cannot do portraits. Somebody once asked me to do a portrait of his wife. I worked on it for almost two years, on and off and on and off. But it was no good.

Sculpture portraits are a craft by itself. To do a portrait it has to look like you and be alive. It's not even enough that it *looks* like you – you want to talk to it and you want it to speak to you. I've tried to do such portraits, but I lose interest, because to me, it's not really creative.

People come to me to do their portraits because I'm well known. I've had commissions to do the portraits of King Hussein and Yitzak Rabin. I gave these to a sculptor in Israel who, I think, is fantastic with portraits but he is unknown. I was very happy to give these to him.

All artists think they have talent, even if they don't have any. Sometimes I see a piece of art and wonder what the artist tried to do. Is the chair a piece of art or is the chair meant for sitting? Some of my chairs are deliberately pieces of art. They're not to sit on, but they are still chairs. But I also have to make chairs that are my breadwinners. They're flatter and more comfortable and have a pillow.

You have to decide what you want to do. There are many ways of being creative. Even if you're not an artist, you can do something else that is creative such as volunteering in a hospital or helping out in countries where people are suffering.

> Don't be afraid. Just try to be yourself. Learn from your mistakes.

For me, helping somebody is the happiest moment of my life. I recently got a call from a friend that an Arab child, four years old, lost his leg and his hand from a bomb that some Arabs were making to use in Israel but that blew up right where they were. Supporting this poor, helpless kid for whom nobody else cared is the kind of thing that makes me happier than anything else.

I try to help as much as I can. But I do it on my own, not as part of a group or any organization. Because when you're with other people, it's wasting time. It's all right to talk and laugh and eat with them, but when you do something on your own, you start really thinking and new ideas are developed.

Never be afraid to be creative

This is my life. I don't know any other life. I have to create. I have to get up in the morning and do something that I love to do and make the day interesting. How much can you travel? How much can you shop? How many restaurants can you visit?

I only know how to live with art, to be surrounded by it. I do this without having had any formal schooling. I instinctively know what I like and what I don't like. I want to be free. I want to get up and go out in the morning and say, "Okay, which way am I going to go today? To the right or to the left?" And then just follow the day.

I would like to teach other people to think like me – not to be afraid, to just go by feeling. Don't be afraid of an old piece of furniture that you have. Don't be afraid of changing it by adding some color to it or making it more contemporary looking. Don't try to do what is fashionable.

I feel good with my clothes. I wear what I like. Some people like things with names like Gucci or Ralph Lauren. I never did. I never follow fashion. I try to dress very classy with a lot of jewelry that I designed.

I always say to people, "Don't be afraid. Just try to be yourself. Learn from

Ilana Goor with hybrid statues she created for the 2006 exhibition at the Tel Aviv museum. *Courtesy of Ilana Goor*

your mistakes." It takes a long time to influence people to just follow their intuition because many people are so insecure.

I have tried to be influential. I believe that my biggest influence has been through my museum. I can see it when I come to some other homes. I can always see my touch there.

When I built my museum in Jaffa, I found old stones at a 400-year-old church in Bethlehem and brought them to Jaffa. Some were so big that we had to cut them to make them fit in the museum. And now people use a lot of stone in their homes. They may not be able to find the kind of stone that I used in my museum but they look for something similar. So, I taught them not to be afraid of using raw material.

Some people cannot afford to buy my table and they may look for something similar. I don't care – I feel that I touched them and I am pleased that I did.

I say to myself, "Ah, they took this idea from my kitchen. Or they took this idea from my bedroom. Or they used the same stone. Good, I taught them not to be afraid."

To know that I influenced someone to be like me, to be happy and enjoy life even if only for a moment, and never to be afraid of trying something new, is the most satisfying and the most creative thing in my life.

KEN HEYMAN

Seeing more than others see

Ken Heyman has published forty books of photographs. During his forty-five years in the photography field, he has completed 150 assignments for Life *magazine, and has been a full member of Magnum. For twenty years he was the photographer for Margaret Mead, the distinguished anthropologist. He has photographed in more than sixty countries and the photos have appeared in major exhibits and two books co-authored with Margaret Mead. His many awards include The World Understanding Award, given "to honor the photographer whose work has contributed most to a better understanding among the world's people."*

I have no choice about being creative. It's part of me.

When I was a young boy at school, I was a poor student because I couldn't memorize names and dates. I didn't know it at the time, but I was substantially *visual* – my visual sense is more than all my other senses combined.

Today, I am a photographer. I photograph people. I see them move and I read their body language. Margaret Mead, whom I worked with for over twenty-three years, described me to a friend by saying, "Ken photographs relationships."

My early influences

Life magazine's first issue came out when I was six years old. At that time my mother kept a scrapbook of cutout pictures from *Life*. Surprisingly, my photographs resemble those in my mother's scrapbooks.

We had paintings around our house – good ones – and much of the conversation was about art, and how important art was, and how important books were. All of this has influenced me.

Even in my early years I was busy *seeing* things. My parents were social and had friends over for dinner once or twice a week. At breakfast the next morning, my mother seemed fascinated by my description of the people who were there the night before. And it reinforced my looking deeply at people.

There is one other thing that may have affected my *seeing*. We were wealthy

Ken Heyman. *Photo: Aronow*

and I was brought up by a nanny – an Irish woman – and she would bring me to the head of the stairs before meeting people and say with an Irish brogue, "Kenneth, just remember, children should be seen and not heard." What I heard her say was, "Children should see and not be heard." I don't know how much that influenced me but her always saying that may, in fact, have reinforced my ability to see.

My parents were older. I was the youngest and the last of a generation. My father was forty years old when I was born and he wasn't interested in children anymore, so I was isolated. My hobbies saved me – model trains and collecting butterflies, matchbook covers, stamps – but eventually photography became my hobby.

> ... my visual sense is more than all my other senses combined.

Wendy, my first wife, and I had an antiques store, and one of our family expressions was, "Ken does windows." It was easy for me to place objects in a space like a store window to make them look attractive. Today I realize that this skill is evident in my photographs, and making a composition is an important part of being a professional photographer.

My first exhibit was at Limelight in New York City's Greenwich Village. Limelight was a special place for young photographers. It was a coffee shop and the only place that exhibited photographs. In 1958, photography was a non-collectable art, and the photographs were for sale at Limelight for $25–100. So I was thrilled when Helen Gee, Limelight's owner, asked me to exhibit my work.

Robert Frank's book of photography, *The Americans*, had just been published and he was a hero to young photographers. He came into Limelight one day and walked through my little exhibit that was hanging at the time. He started to walk out the door when I rushed after him and said, "Robert, I'm Ken Heyman, and those were my photographs you just saw." He barely looked at me and said, "Not good enough." Those were the best words to be expressed to me at that time. From that day on, "not good enough" was my *mantra*.

My work with Margaret Mead

Margaret Mead had a great influence on me. I learned more from her than I did at Columbia University. When I talk to students, one of the things that I tell them is that when they get into college, particularly graduate school, it's a helpful thing to hang around with a professor who is dealing with the problems of the world and doing something about it.

She was my teacher – I worked with her for twenty-three years. She would ask me in September whether I would be free to work with her in January, so

Marilyn Monroe and Arthur Miller on their wedding day. *Photo: Ken Heyman*

that I could fit it into my work schedule. She was not always teaching, but she was a force, a dynamic genius of a woman who helped shape my world view.

I met Dr. Mead when I returned to Columbia after spending two years in the army. She was the most famous professor on campus. Her first class was a lecture course attended by 500 people. When I got to know her well later on, she told me, "That's to make money for Columbia."

On the first day of the class, I sat in the back row up in the bleachers. A little woman came out, plain-looking and pear-shaped, and she began talking… I was spellbound.

At the next class she said, "I can't read all your papers. But if any of you want to add interesting photographs to your paper, I would like that." It was a one-assignment class. There was no homework but one major paper that was due at the end of the term, which entailed a study of a group other than your family.

At the time, I was interested in social work and was working at a Harlem settlement house with tough eight- and nine-year-old boys. So I turned in my assignment with 4×5-in. pictures of them and my comments about their behavior. It was the first time that I realized that you could use your hobby for a real purpose.

At the end of the year, she called me into her office, and suddenly I was face to face with Margaret Mead. I was speechless. She had my book of the Harlem boys on her lap, and said, "Next term, I want you to attend my class in graduate school." I said, "I can't do that, I'm not a graduate student." She said, "Oh, don't be silly. I'll see that you get in."

The book was my first A! Later, she instructed me, "Ken, when we're together, call me Margaret, but in public call me Dr. Mead." She was tough, always moving quickly and a dynamo. When she phoned, she never said "Hello" or "Goodbye." She would speak quickly and hang up the phone. She was unique.

The graduate class was with older professional types – at that time I was an undergraduate. They were anthropologists and psychiatrists, and the course was called "Field Methods and Techniques." In other words, these people were going to go out in the world on anthropological field trips and this course was where they were going to learn what to do.

An experiment was set up with one of the women from the class who had a child about two years old. The students had desks in a semi-circle with an open space at the center. The mother sat in a chair in the middle with her child on the floor. My job was to take photographs and we observed her as if she were from some foreign culture that we had never known. The class took notes on the behavior.

Margaret Mead in Bali 1958. *Photo: Ken Heyman*

The following week, the mother was back and everybody talked about what they had observed. At the end of the class Dr. Mead said, "Ken, I know you were taking pictures, but do you also want to say something?" I said, "I disagree with everybody! Ordinarily, this mother would never have remained in a chair with her child crying on the ground. She would either get on the ground with the child, or lift the child up onto her lap." At that, I heard a noise in the back of the class. It was this mother laughing, and she said, "Ken is absolutely right, but Dr. Mead told me I should stay in the chair."

I was in therapy at the time and, a few hours later, when I was with my therapist, I said, "Is it possible that people see at different levels?" And the therapist said, "Of course, you see much more than most people."

Several months later, Margaret Mead asked me to go to Bali with her as her assistant, just the two of us. It was so enormous that I actually didn't hear her ask me, and that night I woke up thinking, "Did I dream it? Did she actually ask me?" I wasn't sure, so I called her the next morning and said, "Dr. Mead, did you ask me to go to Bali with you?" "Yes, goddam it, and by your not answering, I thought you didn't want to go." "Oh no, of course I want to go." "Well, meet me Thursday six o'clock at my home."

That's the way it started. But I was frightened – what would I talk about with this genius when we got to Bali? I was not much of a conversationalist.

As it turned out, instead of discussion while we worked during the day, we used mealtimes to discuss what happened, and I could ask such things as "Why did the baby have a white spot on his forehead?"

For the first few days, she directed me on picture situations and what to take. After that she just let me go. She would sit in the background while I was taking more pictures than I ever took because I wanted to cover everything, and I was on an exciting, creative high.

Margaret Mead was all business. She was not big with compliments and she never told me my work was good. But she gave me the opportunity to accompany her again, and that was more than a compliment.

Together, we did a book called *Family*, which really helped to give my career a boost because it was a Book of the Month Club alternate and sold over a quarter of a million copies.

Using my photography to educate

Some years later, when my oldest daughter was about to be a student at the Dalton School in Manhattan, and I was in Nigeria on assignment for *Life* magazine, I had a dream about teaching courses in perception. I spent two days writing out a possible high school course. The premise was to encourage visual awareness, and to do homework that did not require reading and writing essays.

When I returned to New York, I showed my typed notes to the principal of the Dalton School. Three days later he said, "Ken, I'd like you to start teaching next week." At the time, Dalton was an all-girls school, and he described the senior class I would be teaching: "These are wealthy young women who are terribly bright and will all go to college, and so there are two things on their minds: one is boys and the other is getting into a college of their choice."

I explained that I didn't have a graduate degree. But the principal said, "I don't care, I want you to teach what you described. And I want to have the school psychologist sit in the class." Maybe this was because he was concerned how the students would respond to my innovative teaching. But the psychologist turned out to be a quiet woman who sat in the back and rarely said anything.

I called the class "Perception and Seeing." The students were smarter than I expected, and they kept me on my toes. There were many projects and, for one of the projects, I spoke about anthropology and how I had worked with Margaret Mead.

I described to the students how all over the world, people live in villages. I said to them, "*You* live in a village." When they looked shocked, I explained, "Your village is your apartment house. I would like you to study your village." I talked about "informants," explaining that informants are important, because they are the persons who bring you into their society. I said, "The informant may be a friend, the doorman or the guy who collects the garbage. Talk to them and say you have a school project, and you want to know which families would be open to being interviewed."

That turned out to be a successful experiment and some of the students even took Polaroid pictures of the families they interviewed.

Exhilarating moments

Once in a while, at my level of photography, something totally unexpected happens as I'm taking pictures. Let me give you an example.

I had to photograph a birth for the beginning of a major photography book. I found a birthing clinic in Manhattan, spoke to the expecting parents and went to the birthing clinic at two o'clock in the morning. I thought I shouldn't use flash but just have soft lights in the room – and, as I was setting up my lights, I blew out the fuse. Everything went black while a nurse went to change the fuse.

When the lights came on, the mother had taken off her clothes, the father had taken off his shirt, and the baby was starting to come out. Suddenly it was like an Adam and Eve situation. At that moment – in this white room with a white bed – I felt extreme excitement, pleasure or whatever. It was like a home run because it was such a basic situation. To make matters even stranger and more exciting, the woman was on all fours rather than on her back, and dropping the baby from her backside with the midwife catching it. It's moments like these that are exhilarating for a photographer.

Up to that point, I had become bored with photography. *Life* and *Look* magazines had closed and I hadn't been photographing much.

Hemingway photographed in Cuba. *Photo: Ken Heyman*

How I changed the way I work

I made a major change in my photography in 1984 when I was one of a hundred photographers on a project, called *A Day in the Life of Canada*. Among all these professionals with all that equipment hanging around their necks, I noticed that a couple of them had this new plastic camera – a "point and shoot" – that I hadn't heard about. Since I don't read photography magazines, I asked an editor friend about this kind of camera. He said, "Buy one," and I knew him well enough to know that I should buy one.

A few days later, when I was driving on Sixth Avenue and had this "point and shoot" loaded with film, I saw a pickup truck full of noisy high school kids who had apparently won some game. So without thinking, I took this camera, put it out the window, pushed the button and took a picture. A few blocks later I thought, "Oh, my God, it's automatic. You don't have to think. Just aim and push. That's incredible!"

I was fascinated by this new "hipshot" kind of photography. My *hobby* of photography came back to me.

On weekends, I used a particular technique. I would put my little "point and shoot" on the ground, or on my side, just snapping pictures. I was taking photographs by not looking through the viewfinder. That brought a new excitement. The photographs on the contact sheets showed situations that I had never seen in photography before, where the foreground was greatly enlarged and the background was shrunk down to mini people because of the very low angle. I had been a photography editor as well as a photographer, but I never saw this kind of distortion before. Suddenly it was "Eureka!" – I had fallen on something that had never been done before.

Up to that point, I had become bored with photography. *Life* and *Look* magazines had closed and I hadn't been photographing much. I was enjoying time with my children and not thinking about photography.

I had previously been working primarily with *Life* magazine – I did over 150 assignments for *Life* and several other magazines – and it was always the editor telling me what to do and describing what was wanted. My job was to bring back images that told a deeper kind of picture story. Working for editors was a culture where I behaved like I should behave, namely turning in good pictures that the editor could publish. But you couldn't sell distortions to the editor of *Life* magazine.

Suddenly, finding something new was exhilarating. Now I was doing things that I had never done – taking chances by putting cameras in strange places. Then, on the contact sheet, one picture would jump out saying, "Look at me." Using that technique, I did a book called *Hipshot*, where the whole book was photographed without looking through the viewfinder. Most of the pictures were photographed by putting the camera on the ground. The whole book was done with no cropping and everything with a full negative.

The book took me three years to do and in doing it, the artist in me came out. I felt creative.

> As the world is changing, television is influencing the world's traditions more and more.

If you had asked me "What motivates a creative person?" before I found this *hipshot* technique, I would have answered as most magazine photographers would have answered, not really understanding creativity in my work because I simply called it "work." Even when a picture turned out exceptionally well, and people would say, "Oh, that's really creative" – to me, it didn't have that ring.

Now I felt that I was doing things that were creative.

Unexpected influences

I love to travel. When I go out, every turn in the road is an unexpected result. I'm currently writing about a village in Portugal, and how it's a turn on, because the people there are so accessible and so friendly. Here was this old-fashioned village on the Portuguese coast, undiscovered by tourists. Down little cobblestone streets each door is a bright color, and every corner is open to a photogenic situation.

Unfortunately these places are disappearing. As the world is changing, television is influencing the world's traditions more and more.

Many years ago I had photographed a spectacular ceremony with old costumes and decorated llamas in Machu Picchu near Lake Titicaca. More recently, my wife, Judy, and I visited the site to once again see the ceremony. This time, however, when the people came out of church, they were dressed in tuxedos and black dresses adorned with gold jewelry. The dancers were dressed like Dallas Cowboy cheerleaders. We were told they watch CNN and want to be modern like the rest of the world.

Many years ago, when I first started photography, television was not yet influential. Clearly, I wanted to use my photographs to explain the world to other people. In those early years I did three important books about the world – the book called *Family* with Margaret Mead, *The World's Family* and another book called *World Enough*. It was my feeling that I was here to explain the world, because it was so different out there than it was in the United States.

I don't know if my photography books have influenced anybody or taught them how to see and read people more the way I do. But, once in a while, you bump into a rather sweet situation where people have been influenced by what you have done. I remember a young woman who said to me, "Oh, Mr. Heyman, I would spend hours looking over the book *Family* at my grandma's house. I knew then what I wanted to do when I grew up – I wanted to be an anthropologist, and today I am an anthropologist." I'm old enough to get that kind of feedback occasionally and I enjoy it.

Right: Hipshot, Brooklyn with point and shoot at street level. *Photo: Ken Heyman*

KARIM RASHID

Changing the aesthetics of product design

Karim Rashid, a leading designer known worldwide for contemporary design of brightly colored plastic products, has radically changed the aesthetics of product design. Born in Cairo, he studied in Ottowa, Canada, and Milan, Italy, and is now living and working in New York. The over 2,000 objects he has designed include furniture, watches, dinnerware and a wide range of everyday accessories. His work is in the permanent collections of fourteen museums, including the Museums of Modern Art in New York and San Francisco. His experience extends to architecture and interiors, such as the Morimoto restaurant in Philadelphia and the Semiramis Hotel in Athens. He is the recipient of numerous awards, among them the 2006 Pratt Institute Legend Award.

G ood design is based on a set of rules. Great design shapes a moment in time. Most people live a life that follows a kind of existing set of rules or methodologies, and that inevitably leads to just repeating history. To me, this is very unsatisfactory.

The way to change history, or change our present, is by breaking those rules. We are living at a time where our creative ideas are becoming exhausted because the existing environment is saturated with ideas, especially when it comes to commodities and to the physical world. I used to tell my students: "Learn everything you can about a project, and then forget it overnight."

There are great opportunities in the virtual world. It's a new field. It's a new playground. But the physical world is so saturated that we are getting to a point where very little is really original any more. In order to strategically go beyond what exists in the physical environment, we have to start turning things upside down and completely rethinking the way we live, the way we work, the way we play, the way we function.

I am convinced that we are all born creative. Already as children, we have a certain sense of equilibrium and this notion of imagination and wanting to create. Every child picks up a pen or a pencil and sketches and draws. The

Karim Rashid. *Photo: Ilan Rubin*

creative evolution of a human being is that, as a child, you start to draw first from your imagination. Later, you start to imitate the real world and, still later, there's a kind of symbiosis of the real world and the imagination.

This process of development indicates that, in one way or another, we're basically all creative beings. What kind of behavioral or educational conditioning you've had at a young age determines whether or not you continue to be a creative human being.

Sometimes it's your parents, or it could be your environment, or the school you attend. Or it could even be your best friend – you find him drawing cars all the time and before you know it, you're drawing cars as well. There is definitely something about behavioral support that makes us into creative beings.

What made me pursue a creative career?

Obviously, I have some artistic instinct in me. But is this enough to have made me pursue a creative life, a creative career? On the one hand, you can argue that being a creative person is genetic. On the other hand, it could have been my education at home or in school that influenced me to be creative.

I studied design in Ottawa, Canada and graduated with a Batchelor's Degree in Industrial Design. Then I went to Italy for my Master's Degree and, more recently I was awarded an Honorary Ph.D. in Fine Arts at Washington Cortland University.

But is this what made me creative? I'm convinced that, in my particular case, the strongest influence to be a creative person came from my upbringing in a very artistic family.

My father was a painter and a set designer for television programs and our house was full of furniture and lighting that he designed. He would be sketching my mother every night. He would be painting until four in the morning. As a child, he would take me on weekends to see the television sets that he had designed and I would be running around in the studio all the time. So I really grew up in a creative world all that time. Thus, in a sense, I *learned* to be creative and I was *encouraged* to be creative.

> I am convinced that we are all born creative.

My mother taught me how to use a sewing machine when I was seven years old and I sewed my own clothes. Many times, after dinner, instead of watching television, we would sit around the family table and all draw each other. So I was fortunate to be brought up in this very creative environment.

But then, you could argue that there are people out there who are creative without growing up in creative surroundings. A friend of mine, a brilliant violinist, had parents who were both doctors. So she was not brought up in a really creative environment. Nevertheless, there was probably some kind of creative outlook that the parents had, even if they weren't conscious of it. It may be how they lived their lives or perhaps they saw the world in a different way than other people saw it.

> Creative thought is really based on human and social behavior.

I firmly believe that it's the formative years that shape a child and whether the child will grow up to be creative for the rest of his or her life. But there's also a certain kind of laziness that's part of the human condition. The majority of us are lazy. Especially, as we get older, we focus more and more on making a living and on various activities that seem to be most important to us, and being creative takes a back seat.

If, lets say, we go to school to study dentistry, we soon forget the pleasure of picking up a sketch pad, as we did as a child, making a sketch, or a drawing, or thinking about building something when we get home. Once we're busy in our daily activities, the next thing that happens is that we become more and more occupied with our career and less and less interested in the notion of creating.

Unfortunately, today's society tends to suppress creativity. Society teaches us to conform – in school, at home, at a restaurant, at a ball game – in short, everywhere. So here you are as a child, all creative and full of ideas, and the next thing you know, you grow up among a conforming society. Conforming at a young age prevents the majority of people, who may be basically creative, from pursuing a creative career.

Creative thought is really based on human and social behavior. In a lot of my work I study – and, I have to admit, almost obsessively – human behavior. No matter where I am at any time, I find myself observing people.

Because my work is international, I am often on a plane and even there I find myself studying everything all the time – the way someone is holding a coffee cup, the way someone is talking to a flight attendant, how the chairs on the plane move, everything around me. So, that way I'm perpetually absorbing as much as I can about the existing environment. At the same time, I'm ready to break all those rules.

My field of activity is mainly industrial design, although my range may be a bit broader than that of the typical industrial designer. A lot of my projects are assignments and each assignment has various criteria and mandates. For instance, I've designed a line of men's hair grooming products – combs, brushes and things like that. I was given a very specific strategic set of criteria: "This is the kind of market that we are aiming for. These are the price points

Alessi Kaj Watch. *Courtesy of Karim Rashid Inc.*

we are aiming for," and so forth. Sometimes there's even discussion of the typology of the marketplace, such as "We are going after the metrosexuals."

I don't really believe in a lot of these mandates. I'm a big believer that good design crosses all those boundaries, so that if you do something really good, it can be as appropriate for a ten-year-old as for an eighty-year-old person. In other words, I believe that good design is a universal language.

However, in industrial design, you frequently have to work within very tight requirements. I'm often given assignments where there is a very specific target group. For example, if a cosmetics company comes to me to design a cosmetics line, they may give me a mandate that is primarily based on functional, practical things such as the cost of production, the requirement of glass, or the volume of the object.

Another cosmetics company may prefer to give me, let's say, the scent. This is much broader because I can work off the scent and can be more poetic because, at the end of the day, it's the bottle that communicates the "personality" of the scent that's inside.

Other times, there is the opportunity to work on a broader scale of design when someone, possibly from a furniture company, may say to me, "Do anything you want. Come up with ideas. Let's look at ideas." I'm consulting on an automobile design right now. The assignment is to do a conceptual car and there are very few criteria. They are looking for ideas and I can go in almost any direction I choose.

Another assignment where I was given a very broad design opportunity was from a mobile phone company. This company's only criteria were the sizes of the LCD display, the circuit board and the battery pack. The rest was up to me. I didn't have any material level, production level or anything else. They basically said, "Do anything you want."

So there are extremes in direction. What I've learned in the years of being a designer is that the more mass-produced a product is, the tighter are usually the criteria. When a product is more at the luxury end, or if it has lower volume production, it tends to be more wide open.

Every designer has a different agenda and different creative goals. My agenda is that I need to do something original or I don't sleep at night. I'm concerned about the originality of a design assignment the second someone tells me about the project. Every project I work on must have some nuance of originality. The nuance could be that I find a new production method, or a new function, or a new material, or a new look. But for me, there needs to be some level of originality.

As I said earlier, it's getting harder and harder today to do anything really original. That's why I use the word "nuance," because I believe that, more often than not, we are evolving our world these days through subtle changes rather than through drastic changes.

Many designers don't necessarily feel the same way. A lot of them seem to feel that they can reappropriate history without a problem. They seem to be satisfied with reapplying old ideas with a few minor modifications. There's so much commodity in this world today. It seems almost as if some designers think "Why bother? Why fight when a client will be satisfied with a look-alike design?"

To me, every project is, in a way, like giving birth to a child. If you're going to bring up a child, hopefully you'll bring up an intelligent one, one who learns to think for him or herself.

On the other hand, it's very difficult to put anything in the market these days that is completely novel, completely unexpected. This has become a virtual impossibility. The principles of production alone are bound to bring something familiar into play. The minute you talk about any kind of material that we know of and use, it is already familiar.

This is especially true in the United States market, vis-à-vis the European market. I remember, when I was a student in the 1970s, there was a French marketing guru

> My agenda is that I need to do something original or I don't sleep at night.

who spent a lot of years with Procter & Gamble. I remember him showing us two pie charts and he alleged that in America, 97 percent of anything that is in the market has to be familiar to the consumer, while 3 percent new will be acceptable. In Western Europe, he claimed, it was more like 92 percent familiar versus 8 percent new. My feeling is that it's probably more like 80/20, or 90/10.

But today's market is changing a great deal. Today, acceptance of new things is almost an expectation, whereas twenty years ago it was very much a "take no risk" business philosophy, where every company took the safe road by simulating what already existed. That's why so many products looks the same today.

What motives people to be creative?

Motivation is really different from creativity. Creativity is in you. Motivation is what drives you.

You can be a very creative person, but be completely lazy, or not encouraged, without self-motivation. Personally, I am very motivated. Even if I were not a creative person, I would be motivated in a different way. This, I believe, goes back to my childhood again. I was motivated when I was already in primary school. I realized I was a smart kid and decided that I was going to accelerate my education and skip years of school.

So I put a lot of pressure on myself. I had to have the highest marks in every class that I attended. At the age of ten, I was motivated to get home after school, spend two hours to do all my homework, get everything done, memorize everything I needed to do, and then go out and play. I'm not really sure where all this motivation came from.

I believe deeply in the concept of Maslow's "hierarchy of human needs" and I scaled all those levels of his hierarchal pyramid. I started out where it was a way of survival. To survive, I used my creativity to try and achieve security, to get a job, to feed myself. The next level was to be accepted socially as a designer. Then came the level of self-esteem, to get some accolades and build my ego, the ego nurtured by people patting me on the back and telling me that I am good.

But the real aspiration inside me has always been to reach the top of Maslow's pyramid – self-actualization – the realization of my career as a creative person, becoming a successful designer.

I admit that this is completely egocentric. It's about the idea that I need to do creative things and create the built environment. That is part of me – that is somehow in my subconscious.

On the other hand, I still vacillate sometimes between pure creativity and being professionally successful. Deep, deep down in me, left over from my childhood, I have this obsession of just drawing, creating and seeing things manifested, regardless of whether there's a client tomorrow or not, or whether I'm being paid or not.

From sketchpad to worldwide assignments

I was born in Cairo, Egypt. I traveled a lot as a child – we moved from Cairo to Rome, from Rome to Paris, and from Paris to London. When I was seven we went from London to Montreal on the *Queen Elizabeth*.

A lot of those young influences and all the different cultures probably influenced my perspective on what I do today. My activities are very global. I am

Bonaldo Dragonfly Chair. *Courtesy of Karim Rashid Inc.*

working in twenty-nine countries, often on as many as eighty-five projects. I'm not a foreigner anywhere anymore. And I'm incredibly organized. That may also have to do with the place where I was born at a certain date and time, and that I'm a Virgo. I love what I call the "shrinking world" and the fact that I'm part of it all.

As a result of the broad experience that I've had since childhood – in different countries, with different people, different customs and different perspectives – I'm also very broad at what I do creatively. At this point of time, I have four fine art shows going and I'm doing some of those installations. I'm doing product design; I'm designing some jewelry; I'm doing a line of high-heeled shoes for women; I'm designing bathing suits in Korea; and I'm doing several hotels such as the Semiramis Hotel that I did in Greece some time ago. Every project has a different set of criteria and, therefore, a different creative approach and a different work process.

Fessura Bondage. *Courtesy of Karim Rashid Inc.*

When doing all these, I follow a series of steps. I do a lot of flying, so that's a time when I'm alone, and I really need to be alone to draw and think. Again, that goes back to childhood. I used to sit with a sketchpad and draw for four or five hours without ever looking up – I was very focused and I still am. So for me to be really disciplined and in focus, I need to be alone with no distractions – just with the sketchpad and drawing. I generally fill up a sketchpad of a hundred pages or more before I feel really comfortable that I have the right solution or direction.

After the sketch stage, I sit with my senior staff, show them my sketches and tell them about my ideas. Then, after listening to their opinions and their feelings about them, we edit them down to maybe five, six, or seven best ideas. These will be put on the computer so that we can start seeing them in 3-D.

There was a time when I used to do all this honing myself. Now I have several very good people on my staff to help me do this. I have a fine artist, a graphic designer, several engineers and two interior designers. So it's a good mix of creative people. Their contributions include defining and refining my ideas, doing the computer-aided drawings, handling the presentation renderings and a lot of other follow-up tasks.

From time to time, I'll look over their shoulders and suggest that we need to think about this or that. Every day I'll review about five or six different projects with my staff. During any week, I end up reviewing about thirty or forty projects.

The design development of the "Dirt Devil" hand-held vacuum cleaner, for example, is typical of how we proceed through a project. It began, as usual, with my doing about 150 sketches. I reviewed all these drawings with my senior staff and, after pointing at several designs that I thought to be the best ideas, we broke off and three or four people started putting the selected designs on their computers to get the proportions right. They took the motor for the vacuum cleaner that our client gave us and started to build the shell around it.

After we developed and refined six or seven strong ideas, we made rapid prototype models on our prototyping machine in the office. With this machine, you can make plastic 3-D models overnight in about eight hours. So, on the following day, I could actually feel the prototype models in my hand and feel the sense of the scale, the comfort and the proportion. Then we went back to the computer to make some further improvements before presenting the models to our client.

> I believe that well-designed products can have a tremendous influence on people's lives.

Normally, if a client of ours loves two or three of our concepts, we go back and do more detailing on each of the selected prototypes. In the case of the "Dirt Devil," we showed the exact location of the vent holes, the parting lines of the plastic, and a few other such details. The client then produced several of what they call "visual models" that look exactly like the real thing to show to their marketing team and get comments from a few potential buyers.

The next step is for our client's inhouse engineering department to produce the final product. I will usually be involved in approving it and, if needed, making changes on their engineering drawings. Now we have a working prototype with a motor and everything in it to try out to make sure that everything works.

Frequently, my clients ask me to design the packaging for products that I designed – the graphics, the logo, the copy and sometimes even the name of the product, to give the project a totally cohesive image.

This is the element that I love about my work – doing something that is completely mine. Then, when I've completed the project and I look at it, there's often a kind of euphoric, almost phenomenological moment of seeing the project as a whole and I'm really proud and feel great about it.

But, whatever the assignment, the first, and often the most exciting, part of the process is when I start conceptualizing with a pen in my hand. That has not really changed over the years. In a virtual world, it will be nice when I get rid of the pen and just wave my hand. Since that's not likely to happen very soon, I continue to enjoy filling my sketchpad with my Pilot Fineliner.

Another project I did recently was for Method Home USA, a young startup company in San Francisco, which decided that they really wanted to get an enhanced laundry detergent into the market. I was a little skeptical about the whole idea at first, because they have to compete against the really big players in the world of detergents, such as Procter & Gamble. But they had some very strong ideas, and they wanted to bring me in as kind of creative director to design their products to be different from other products in the market. I did that, and it has been a phenomenal success.

The reason I accepted this assignment from a startup company is that I'm always interested in working on something new instead of something that I've already done. I think that's the very nature of creative people.

I believe that well-designed products can have a tremendous influence on people's lives. Think about how the iPod or the RAZR phone has affected people. All these products that we use every day have an enormous effect. They are very powerful and they contribute enormously to shaping our lifestyle. They have the ability to make people's lives better and more productive. You can bring a lot to the human psyche through design. I think design shapes not only our everyday lives and our built environment, but it shapes culture.

My goal is to really do things that are more and more original. I've been very conscious of a pattern in my life. When I started in my twenties, I was working in a design office. That was a period of a lot of learning and also a lot of almost imitating. But I think that's how we learn. We begin to learn through copying. What I was producing at that time was not original. I was just being competent, doing my job, trying to do the best possible work.

When I got to my thirties, I opened my own practice. By that time, I started to have a really strong feeling that I could contribute to the world not just by being another good designer, or another practical person, but by actually doing some really original things.

Now, in my mid-forties, I find that my work has become very much me. Many people now say that they can recognize a Karim Rashid product. I've developed, so to say, my own signature.

This is not always easy because I often have to work with criteria that are so restrictive that it leaves little opportunity to be me. If I'm designing something as banal as a coffee mug, I have to ask myself, "Am I doing just another coffee mug? Is doing this coffee mug just an evolution from what exists? Is there any room for self-expression?"

It has become more and more important to me that in my work I can express myself.

I'm finding that, in almost everything I create these days, I've become more obsessed than ever with who I am. Why am I different from the next person? How does my work differ from that of other designers? Am I really doing things that are different from what already exists? By asking myself these questions, I push myself rigorously to do more original work.

In the next ten years, my goal is to do more original products and architecture – things that no one has ever done before. This may sound very egocentric and it may well be.

But my sincere and deepest hope is that I will be able to create things for the six billion people on this earth that they will find to be meaningful and inspiring.

Semiramis Hotel, Athens, Greece. *Photo: Jean Francois Joussand*

ACKNOWLEDGMENTS

This book, as all creative endeavors, required a substantial amount of research and interviews. Many of the individuals we interviewed put aside a large chunk of their busy schedules for us. We are deeply grateful to those who contributed their time and attention in providing us with information for this book.

We are also especially thankful to a long list of individuals who helped us in making contacts, reviewing parts of the manuscript, making helpful suggestions and providing the photographs that accompany the chapters. They include:

Jakob Holder, assistant to Edward Albee; Jochen Frey, BMW Group, Corporate Communications; Kristina Weith, BMW Group, Product and Technology Communication; Tom Philipp Peters, BMW Group, Corporate Communications; Janet Makela, Chihuly Studio; Ken Clark, Chihuly Studio; Jean Halberstam; Kim Gerstman, director of Major Gifts, ACLU; Ken Fernandez, Research and Archives, Pace Wildenstein; Carol Weiner, publications manager, Pace Wildenstein; Jon Mason, director, Research and Archives, Pace Wildenstein; David Marx, attorney; Len Lowengrub; Irina Steger, receptionist, Porsche Design Studio; Angela Sibold, PR, Porsche Lizenz-& Handels; David van de Leer, Public Relations & Exhibitions, Steven Holl; Lisetta Koe, Think Tank New York IIC; Sara Roberts, assistant to Erica Jong; Ralph Wharton, clinical professor, Columbia University; Charlotte White; Jackie Bazan, CEO, Bazan PR; Jason R. Lampkin, 40 Acres administrative supervisor; Thierry Debaille, director of scheduling, Studio Daniel Libeskind; Jessica Scaperotti, PR, Studio Daniel Libeskind; Vinay Rao, Office of the CEO, Infosys; Peter McLaughlin, group manager, Public Relations North America, Infosys; Jessica M. Pearson, PR and Communications, Karim Rashid; Beverly Coe, assistant to James Rosenquist; Michael Harrigan, curator, James Rosenquist Inc.; Jules Cazedessus, production coordinator, Julie Taymor; Allen Gardner, executive assistant, Cooper-Hewitt, National Design Museum; Julie Roebuck, executive assistant to Steve Wozniak; Melissa Eagan, executive producer, The Leonard Lopate Show; Winfrida Mbewe, publicity manager, WW Norton; Elizabeth Hunt, transcriptions.

We would also like to thank the publishing staff at Palgrave Macmillan, specifically Steve Rutt, Alexandra Dawe, and Isobel Munday; and extend our appreciation for the page layout work by Linda Norris, Aardvark Editorial Ltd.

Last and certainly not least, no efforts in connection with this book should ignore the patience of our beloved spouses for sharing our time and attention with the book's creation. We believe that they will ultimately participate in our pride in presenting *Creativity: Unconventional Wisdom from 20 Accomplished Minds* to our readers.

4 Week L~~
This book is

F